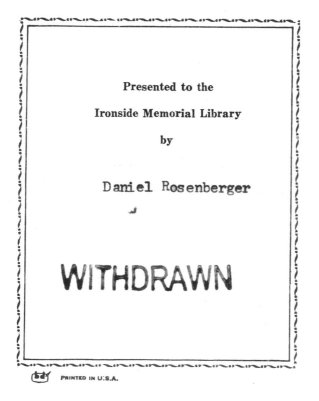

Galbraith Hall Todd is the deserving successor of Dr. Clarence Macartney in the pulpit of the Arch Street Presbyterian Church in Philadelphia.

Dr. Todd received his higher education at Westminster College and Princeton Theological Seminary. Since 1948 he has been Lecturer in Homiletics at the Reformed Episcopal Seminary in Philadelphia.

Before coming to Philadelphia Dr. Todd served the Pierce Avenue Presbyterian Church at Niagara Falls, New York. He is a contributor to the *Colliers' Encyclopedia*. He is the author of numerous articles and his sermons have appeared in print from time to time.

With this background Dr. Todd is well equipped to furnish a book of graphic, Scripture-based sermons for the Easter season. His *Seven Words of Love* is already in its second printing.

THE GAMBLERS AT GOLGOTHA

G. HALL TODD

THE GAMBLERS AT GOLGOTHA

1957
BAKER BOOK HOUSE
Grand Rapids, Michigan

THE GAMBLERS AT GOLGOTHA

Library of Congress Catalog Card Number: 57-14757

PHOTOLITHOPRINTED BY CUSHING - MALLOY, INC.
ANN ARBOR, MICHIGAN, UNITED STATES OF AMERICA

Contents

1

The Donor of the Donkey

> *"And as they were loosing the colt, the owners thereof said unto them, Why loose ye the colt? And they said, The Lord hath need of him."* LUKE 19:33, 34

In that stirring tale, Ben Hur, Iras tells the hero of the story, "I saw your dreaming Caesar make His entrance into Jeursalem. You told us He would that day proclaim Himself King of the Jews from the

steps of the Temple. I beheld the procession descend
the mount bringing Him. I heard their singing. They
were beautiful with palms in motion. I looked everywhere among them for a figure with a promise of
royalty — a horseman in purple, a chariot with a
driver in shining brass, a stately warrior behind an
orbed shield, rivalling his spear in stature. I looked
for his guard. It would have been pleasant to have
seen a prince of Jerusalem and a cohort of the legions
of Galilee. Instead of a Sesostris returning in triumph
or a Caesar helmed and sworded — ha, ha, ha! —
I saw a man with a woman's face and hair, riding
an ass's colt, and in tears. The King! The Son of God!
The Redeemer of the world! — ha, ha, ha!"

Who was the donor of the donkey on which Jesus
rode into the streets of Jerusalem, fulfilling Zechariah's
prophecy?

This unnamed man was evidently one of the
Saviour's unknown friends. He had many friends beyond the circle of His disciples. Their identity was
frequently not known to the disciples. There was
the friend who provided the hospitality of the upper
room. There was the friend, not of the apostolic band,
who performed the beautiful office of anointing Him
for His burial. There was the aristocratic friend, who
at the risk of prestige and position, interceded on
Jesus' behalf with those in high authority. There was
an affluent friend who in the dusk of the day of
the cross offered the untenanted tomb of his garden.

God's cause and kingdom always have unknown,
unsuspected friends. When Israel was pervaded by

the lecherous cult of Baalism and it seemed to Elijah
that he alone remained, the despairing prophet under
the juniper tree had to be reminded that there were
seven thousand loyal, substantial souls in Israel who
had not bowed the knee to Baal.

In the dark day of Absalom's rebellion, it was a
woman unknown to King David, who was instrumental
in saving his life and the lives of his two messengers,
Jonathan and Ahimaaz. In an empty well in her
garden, a peasant woman of Bahurim, faithful to her
king in the time of his distress, concealed his messengers from the surveillance of Absalom's scouts.

Amid the architectural glories of the bustling city
of Corinth, the Apostle Paul lost heart because of the
vices of heathenism which seemed to dominate the
life and thought of the citizenry. He began to believe
that the Christians constituted an inconsiderable and
impotent minority. In a vision of the night, the Lord
cheered the apostle with the assurance, "Be not
afraid . . . for I have much people in this city." God
had loyal hearts and true, if not actual disciples of
Christ, who were not perceived by Paul in Corinth.

One of our younger missionaries in China told me
some years ago that he was touched deeply by a
lowly Chinese woman in a remote village, who, a
stranger to him, came and informed him that she
was praying constantly for him and his labors in
the Lord.

There are persons who sit unobtrusively in our
churches, and it may be, have names that never appear
on the rolls of any of them, yet are friends of the

Lord Jesus. They are quiet, reserved persons, with an affinity of nature for Jesus. They have faith in Christ in their hearts. They make Christ known in the love which permeates their homes. In a subtle but telling fashion they reveal Christ in their business and professional pursuits. They have never been regarded as leaders in the church. They are unrecognized in church circles. There is that about them which indicates that they have a trysting place with Christ. There is about their personalities a distinguishing mark as if they had lived in the high company of Christ. They have sheltered Christ in their kindnesses and philanthropies. They can be expected to support the institutions of mercy and culture which originated in the spirit of Christ and under the inspiration of His teachings. Sometimes their devotion to Jesus goes undetected until a legacy or memorial gift to the church or some related cause, upon which rests the Saviour's blessing, appears as a surprise. Indeed in their post-mortem benefactions they sometimes bless the church and her allied agencies more magnanimously than those who were anticipated to be the church's lavish friends.

The donor of the donkey was a man whose heart the Lord opened. The Master had assured the disciples that their errand would prove successful and they were not chagrined.

Jesus told His disciples of every age what they could expect. As a thorough realist, He sent them forth as sheep in the midst of wolves, warning them that in the world they would have tribulation and that the enmity and hatred which had been visited upon Him would descend upon them. It is not surprising that, as Browning puts it, it is hard to be a Christian.

On the other hand it is an encouragement for the servants of Christ, especially those engaged in the ministry and teaching of His Word to know that the purpose for which they are sent will be accomplished. God does not permit His Word to return unto Him void. The sermon which has been produced under the guidance of the Spirit of God will find persons who have been prepared in mind and heart and made receptive by the selfsame Spirit. When a minister goes on a call in the service and strength of his Master, he can proceed in the glad consciousness that arrangements have been made by the directing hand of God's Spirit. The hearts of men in all stations and not alone of kings are, according to the explicit teaching of the Word of God, in the hand of the Lord as the rivers of water. Jesus assured His disciples that when they were hailed before tribunals or confronted crucial situations to testify on behalf of their convictions, they were to be unconcerned. "Take no thought how or what ye shall speak. ... For it is not ye that speak, but the Spirit of your Father which speaketh in you." When Hugh Latimer went to his martyrdom in England he saluted Nicholas Ridley, his fellow martyr, "Be of good cheer, Brother Ridley, for by the grace of God we shall light in England this day such a candle as will not soon be put out": the cheering thoughts were directed to Latimer's mind not only for his own strengthening of spirit but also to fortify Ridley. Confronted by those who are filled with intellectual bewilderment and skepticism and demand of us, who believe, a reason for the hope that is within us, we can be calm in the thought that there is the presence of the Holy Spirit animating our minds and memories as well as governing our tongues.

The omniscient and sovereign Christ who facilitated the disciples in their task of procuring the donkey for the Palm Sunday procession, is no less in control of events when we discharge His errands today.

The donor of the donkey had possessions of which Jesus stood in need. The philologist, Archbishop Richard C. Trench, in a noble sonnet speaks of Christ in His self-limitation:

Oh, self-restraint, surpassing human thought!
To have all power, yet be as having none!
Oh, self-denying love, that thought alone
For needs of others, never for its own.

Jesus allowed Himself to be placed in need of the service which men could render to Him.

There were many who contributed to the needs of Jesus. Peter gave Jesus the use of his house in Capernaum and that proved to be the setting for many of His miracles of healing. There was a home in Bethany that provided days of retirement and relaxation. Fishing boats were loaned that He might use them as His pulpit. Jesus needed the friendships of His years of earthly ministry. He was afforded the hospitality of the homes of Matthew, Zacchaeus, Simon the Leper, and others.

Christ had needs which friends could supply. He had not where to lay His head, although the armies of heaven were at His disposal.

The rich young ruler had gifts of mind and heart and substance which Jesus might have used. The graciousness of his personality and the amplitude of his wealth would have been of immeasurable help in ministering to the unfortunate. The charming young man was reluctant to place himself at the Master's disposal.

John had depths of affection and a mystical, metaphysical trend of mind which Christ could use. Peter had a vigor and a ruggedness and a commanding personality. Matthew had the precision of a tax collector. Zacchaeus had wealth to share with the less fortunate. Simon the Zealot had the fiery nature and the ardor of the political crusader that could add zest to the apostolic band and preserve Christ's cause from the moribundity of a staid conservatism and traditionalism. Mark had youth and eagerness for action. Luke had medical skill, a trained intellect, and a penchant for the meticulous research of a scientific historian. The ministering women had sympathy and tenderness and undaunted fealty. Mary had the contemplative, pensive nature which makes a responsive listener. Martha had domesticity, culinary proficiency, and a strain of the managerial. Paul had tremendous mental and moral power, a broad education, cosmopolitan horizons from his youth, and an indefatigable spirit.

Augustine had literary grace and philosophical erudition. Constantine had the imperial power needed by Christianity if it were to conquer the world and cease to be a struggling, minority religion. Luther had excellent training and great gusto. Calvin had logic and depth and a classical background. Wesley had the scholarship which would balance his fervor. General Booth had the rugged individualism which would lead him to dare being unconventional. Whitefield had the prodigious vocal power to transmit the message of repentance and faith. Moody had the practical, common sense, homely approach for the businessmen of America and England as he made a straightforward, unadorned appeal, holding before men the goodness and severity of God as disclosed in Christ's atonement. Billy Sunday had the athletic prowess, the histrionic talent, and the ingenious, striking phrases that captivated the imagination of vast, popular audiences across America, leading many to the acceptance of Christ as Saviour, making religion a common if not a favorite topic of conversation in every circle, and directing attention to the scourge of the liquor traffic in the United States.

Everyone has some gift or grace to contribute to Christ and His kingdom. It may be a heart full of compassion and charity. It may be a pleasant, tactful manner. It may be business acumen, charm of personality, the ability to speak, which Aaron long ago devoted to God's cause. It may be the capacity to write well, brilliance of mind, generosity. It may be the grace of making Christ loved and lived in the home. There is no one who lacks the power to be kind.

Everyone has some distinctive contribution to make to Christ and His kingdom in the world.

A nuance made luminous by the Revised Standard Version is this story found in the translation of St. Mark 11:3 — "If any one says to you, 'Why are you doing this?' say, 'The Lord has need of it and will send it back here immediately.' "

Jesus in His own inimitable manner returns the gifts placed at His disposal.

2

A Man Carrying
a Jug of Water

"And he (Jesus) said unto them, Behold, when ye are entered into the city, there shall a man meet you, bearing a pitcher of water; follow him into the house where he entereth in." LUKE 22:10

The man carrying a jug of water was engaged in a menial task. In fact, he was discharging a role usually performed by women in that Oriental world. Many men would have been humiliated beyond measure to procure water for their master's household as did this unnamed man, whom God used as a significant actor in the drama of his only-begotten Son's last week on earth. "All service," wrote Browning, "ranks the same with God."

> A servant with that clause
> Makes drudgery divine;
> Who sweeps a room as to God's laws
> Makes that and the action fine.
> — GEORGE HERBERT

Speaking at the final assembly in Old Council at Oberlin College, Dr. George Walter Fiske, reminiscing concerning that structure, which was one of the earliest buildings of the college and had once housed the school of theology, recalled the tradition that in an early and impecunious day of the college's history, one of the professors spent part of his summer vacation mending the old, well-worn carpets with his own hands, that they might survive another year of hard usage.

There is no task too small, humble, or unworthy for a fitting and honorable place in the plan of God. It is said that Christopher Saur, who in 1743 published the first translation of the Bible in a European language to appear in this country, personally collected soot from the chimneys of houses in Germantown, Philadelphia, in order to produce ink, and gathered old rags for the paper used in the copies of that noteworthy German Bible. Albert Schweitzer, our age's paragon of versatility, is not averse to cleaning the animal pens in the compound of his famous hospital on the edge of the forest primeval. On a dark morning after a shipwreck, the Apostle Paul was seen gathering bundles of sticks for a bonfire by which he and his fellow victims on the island of Malta could obtain some measure of warmth. He, who could earn his livelihood and at the same time produce his profound theological treatises, counted not himself superior to a lowly function in meeting human need.

The man bearing a pitcher of water demonstrates to us that the supreme events in God's kingdom and plan are often hinged on supposedly insignificant, obscure persons. Without this unnamed man, the Last Supper and the institution of the sacrament could not have been. Little, forgotten men and women are often pivotal in cardinal, strategic events. The decisive battle is contingent upon the heroism and fidelity of the common soldier. A policeman faithful to duty and strolling in a Washington alley might have prevented the assassination of Abraham Lincoln on that Good Friday night in Ford's Theatre. He might have intercepted a mad actor's nefarious plot. It was the protests of a humble woman in his first parish in the Netherlands that weighed heavily in the thinking of a young Dutch Reformed pastor named Abraham Kuyper and forced him to re-examine the rationalism and skepticism with which he had been imbued in his theological education. This lowly woman's restrained rebuke concerning his anti-supernaturalistic attitude towards the Bible and the doctrines of the faith, combined with the reading of the now forgotten English novel, *The Heir of Redcliffe,* caused Kuyper to ponder his beliefs and turn to the theological orthodoxy of which he became so renowned a champion at the height of his varied career as a Calvinistic theologian, educator, journalist, and prime minister of Holland.*

In your life it may have been some undistinguished Western Union messenger, who delivered a message, or some unknown telephone operator, who expedited the call, which changed the direction of your life.

Jesus instructed the disciples as they prepared to observe the Passover that they should find at a certain public fountain a manservant bearing a pitcher of water. Although he would give no evidence of recognizing them, they were to follow him until he turned and faced them at the threshold of his master's house. The arrangements were veiled in secrecy because of the conspiracy of Judas. Had Judas been conversant with the Saviour's advance plans, He might have prompted the priests to have Jesus seized and arrested in the midst of the Last Supper. The disciples found that the man with the pitcher of water was at the fountain, and at the moment of their arrival near the fountain he started in the direction of the house where he was employed.

The perfect synchronizing of events in this incident indicates the providential oversight of God. "All things," observed the Apostle Paul, "work together for good." There is a mysterious cooperation of factors in a human situation which transcends the control

*The biographical details are found in *The Reformed Principle of Authority,* by Gerrit H. Hospers.

of human agents. Luke, in his description of the presentation of the infant Jesus in the temple, tells how the aged priest Simeon "came by the Spirit" at the very juncture when Mary and Joseph brought the Holy Child into those hallowed precincts. Anna, the prophetess, came to the temple, as Luke indicates with dramatic emphasis, "in that instant." On the desert highway leading to Gaza, the evangelist Philip arrived at the side of a chariot rolling southward, at the exact moment an official of Ethiopia was reading Isaiah's prophecy of the suffering Messiah. By intimation of the Holy Spirit, Philip drew near and was led to interpret to this man in pensive mood the deep truths of the gospel enshrined prophetically in Isaiah's rhapsodic sentences.

It was a winter's night. A young man in downtown Cincinnati, Ohio, wandered into a stately Episcopal church. He had never before attended a service of that communion. The dress of the clergy, the form of the prayers, the alternate reading of the Psalms gave him the impression of a "reverent and solemn dignity" which he had until then never known. One of the ministers read most impressively an unfamiliar passage, the thirty-sixth chapter of Jeremiah. "The reading," said the young man long thereafter, "swept my soul along as on the winds of imagination into an entirely new region of thought and feeling" (Algernon S. Crapsey of Rochester, N.Y., in his autobiography *The Last of the Heretics,* Alfred A. Knopf, 1924). The Bible henceforth became his constant companion. He looked upon that Sexagesima Sunday night as the date of his conversion, from which he hurried home as in a rapture to read that passage as well as others from the Book with growing enthusiasm.

A minister never knows when some service or sermon or slightest gesture has been designed by Providence to shape the course of someone's career. He never knows as he prepares carefully a sentence in the course of a sermon that God is guiding him to speak that word in season to some unknown individual who will be directed to him, as Cornelius was brought to Peter at Joppa, at a precise moment of need and interest.

The man bearing a pitcher of water is one of the immortal nameless souls of the Bible and history. What a host they are! There are the shepherds, all of whom are unidentified; the Wise Men, whose names are supplied in tradition, but not in Scripture; a certain Samaritan later designated the Good Samaritan; the woman of Samaria, whom Jesus encountered at Jacob's well; the lad, whose picnic lunch of five barley loaves and two small fishes, was multiplied by the Master to feed the hungering crowds; the soldier who ran taking a sponge and filling it with vinegar seeking to assuage the thirst of Jesus; the town clerk of Ephesus, who becalmed the irate mob and saved the Apostle Paul from their savage depredations; the unknown youth, who was responsible for Paul being let down in a basket over the wall, thus escaping the plot against his life; and that company mentioned by the apostle in a suggestive clause as "the rest of my fellow workers, whose names are in the book of life." There was a child at play, whose voice uttering the phrases of a juvenile game, was heard by Augustine at the exact time of his conversion in a Milanese garden, thus figuring unawares in that momentous spiritual experience.

Psychologists write of the pathetic struggle on the part of so many for significance and recognition. The sea of life, as the Brittany fishermen depict it, is so great and our boats are so small. Many must be content with anonymity.

The man with a pitcher of water could have applied to him St. Paul's striking paradox, "unknown, yet well known." With slight alteration in phrasing, the inscription on the monument to the unknown dead of the Civil War at Winchester, Virginia, epitomizes this servant in a house in the Holy City, "who he was, none knows; what he was, all know."

Far better is it to discharge some simple, useful work in the world than to achieve the objective of the builders of Babel, making a name for one's self. After praising famous men and illustrious ancestors, the author of the Apocryphal book of Ecclesiasticus (44:9) alludes to that great company, who are kindred spirits with the man carrying a jug of water:

> "Some there be, which have no memorial: who are perished as though they had not been, and are become as though they had not been born; and their children after them."

Periods of warfare have impressed upon us the vastness of the host of unsung and unknown heroes. Every war has reproduced the situation reported in the Second Book of Samuel, when Joab compiled a casualty list after the battle between the followers of Abner and his chief, Ishbosheth, the son of King Saul, who had been proclaimed by Abner as king over the eleven tribes. In Joab's accounting, "There lacked of David's servants nineteen men and Asahel." Nineteen remained nameless. Only one was cited.

Edward Everett Hale, author of one of the most powerful short stories in the history of American letters, celebrates the nameless heroes and saints:

The unknown good that rest
In God's still memory, folded deep:
The bravely dumb that did their deed,
And scorned to blot it with a name,
    Men of the plain heroic breed
That loved Heaven's silence more than fame.

In the Philadelphia Navy Yard at the confluence of the Delaware and Schuylkill Rivers there is to be seen the U.S.S. Olympia, Dewey's flagship at the Battle of Manila Bay during the Spanish-American War. That vessel, recently threatened with destruction, has an added though often ignored distinction. It was used to convey the body of the Unknown Soldier from France to this country following World War I.

Many have to be resigned to the position of unknown soldiers of the cross. George Eliot concludes *Middlemarch* with her comment concerning Dorothea: "Her full nature like that river of which Cyrus broke the strength, spent itself in channels which had no great name on earth. But the effect of her being on those around her was incalculably diffusive: for the growing good of the world is partly dependent on unhistoric acts; and that things are not so ill with you and me as they might have been is half owing to the number who lived faithfully a hidden life, and rest in unvisited tombs."

One must be satisfied to be unnoted if he has been allowed to accomplish some good, some "little unremembered acts of kindness, the best portion of a good man's life," some service to a cause greater than self. In one of his poems, the American author, Richard Henry Stoddard, speaks of the manner in which a single grape is crushed beyond identification and separate existence to produce the rich, red wine of the chalice. Even so, he indicates, we should be ready in complete selflessness to devote our lives, all unrecognized, to the kingdom of Christ, although not one of God's servants, however unknown to men, is forgotten before Him.

In the background of the careers of men of fame have been uncelebrated men and women whose influence has been mighty.

In his poem, *Each and All*, Emerson refers to a man who was not aware of his own influence and remained unknown by one whom he had influenced.

> The sexton tolling his bell at noon
> Deems not that great Napoleon
> Stops with his horse and lists with delight
> Whilst his files sweep round yon Alpine height.

In 1879 a little-known layman in a Methodist church in Wilmington, North Carolina, asked if he might extend invitations to the services of their church to sailors on the ships anchored in the local harbor. The man went down to the docks, where he found a Chinese cabin boy, named in this country, Charlie Jones Soong. The boy came to the church, embraced the Christian faith, received a Christian education. Returning to his native land he rose to great influence and became the father of a notable family, including Madame Chiang Kai Shek and Madame Sun Yat Sen. Who, alas, can name that Methodist layworker today?

The fame of George Mueller and his orphanage in Bristol, England, has gone through Christendom, yet few know anything about Mueller's young friend, Beta, who, when Mueller was a wayward young man of twenty-one in Germany, took him to the home of a simple, yet devout and earnest Christian, who led him to faith in the Christ, whose promised greater works he later wrought through his phenomenal philanthropies.

Behind the Biblically tinctured, incomparable, literary style of the addresses of Abraham Lincoln is the dim figure of a Virginian, Denton Offut. Disowned by his proud family, highly educated, and, as the result of a strange series of circumstances, he arrived in the frontier Indiana village of New Salem. There he had a library of a thousand volumes, including the great classics. Little did Offut realize that in making his many books available to a young store clerk he was indirectly contributing to the moulding of one of the noblest English styles.

An officer in the church which I formerly served

told how as a Sunday School officer in another Presbyterian church, he had one day enrolled in a Sunday School class two negro boys. One of those boys, R. Nathaniel Dett, who was there instructed in the Christian faith, became the composer of music interpreting the religious faith of his people. His most widely known composition was *Listen to the Lambs.*

As we are called to fulfill tasks for which there is little or no recognition, but which contribute, far above our meager power to compute, to the kingdom of Christ, we should lift the ancient prayer of Moses, "Establish thou the work of our hands upon us; yea, the work of our hands establish thou it."

The man bearing the pitcher of water moved momentarily out of the shadows where he had been a dim figure, such as Rembrandt might have painted. As he came near to the light of Christ for a brief moment, he found eternal significance for his deed. Our lives and our apparently inconsequential deeds become immortal and meaningful as they are related to Christ and the services of His purposes. No less than the greatest in the kingdom and no less than this man, whose act is held in everlasting remembrance, the least we do for Jesus is fraught with deep divine honor and glory and immortality. In a powerful passage in his *History of the French Revolution,* Thomas Carlyle alludes to King Louis XV of France, once much loved, later terribly hated. "Louis was a ruler; but art thou not also one? His wide France — look at it from the fixed stars (themselves not yet infinitude) — is no wider than they narrow brick field, where thou too didst faithfully or didst unfaithfully. Man, symbol of eternity imprisoned into Time! it is not thy works, which are all mortal, infinitely little, and the greatest no greater than the least, but only the spirit thou workest in, that can have worth or continuance."

Rejoice that you are permitted like the man bearing a jug of water to do some humble deed for Jesus and His kingdom, of which there shall be no end.

3

The Host of the Upper Room

"The goodman of the house." MARK 14:14

It is an evidence of our Lord's faithful observance of the cherished traditional forms of the Hebrew religion that we find in the disciples' question to Him, "Where wilt thou that we go and prepare that thou mayest eat the passover?" Jesus accorded a scrupulous respect to the external rites of his ancestral faith.

While He might have pleaded His spiritual transcendence of outward and visible signs and forms that are required by the less mature spiritually, He never did so. "It behooved Him to fulfill all righteousness." He remembered the Sabbath day to keep it holy. He went with uninterrupted regularity on that day to the synagogue. He observed the Passover and the several religious feasts and ordinances, the various means of grace and offices of the religion of the Hebrews.

Jesus indicated that a friend, designated cryptically as "the goodman of the house," had extended to Him and the disciples the hospitality of his spacious home. He offered to them the use of a "large upper room furnished." In the enforced secrecy of the proceedings, so conducted because of the vigilance of His plotting foes, Jesus instructed that the disciples, who comprised a committee on arrangements, should go to a public fountain in Jerusalem and there find a "man bearing a pitcher of water." They were to follow him until he reached the portals of his master's mansion.

The man who provided the upper room in his commodious house had, no doubt, wealth and position. Like Joseph of Arimathaea and Nicodemus, he was probably a patrician and such a person as Galsworthy might have had as a character in one of his novels and Sargent as the subject of one of his portraits. Artists have frequently depicted Christ appearing as a guest in some humble abode of their own period. Perhaps the most familiar of such paintings is that by the German artist, Fritz von Uhde, who pictures humble German peasants standing at the table at their evening meal. As they lift their hearts in grateful prayers, Christ stands in the midst as He did long ago in the home in Emmaus, and there bestows His blessing. Albert William Holden, an English artist of the last century, shows Christ as the guest in the salon of a man of affluence. He stands in the luxurious and stately dining room of a Victorian mansion. In the doorway is a portly, bewhiskered man of dignity and obvious opulence, of whom it could be observed as Samuel Johnson said of Edmund Burke that no one could be in conversation with him many minutes without sensing that he was a man of distinction.

Christ comes to those who are clothed in purple and fine linen and fare sumptuously every day quite as much as to the forgotten man who spends thirty-eight years of frustration, always being thrust aside by others as he waits to plunge his deformed body into the therapeutic waters of Bethesda's pool. The good-man of the house belongs to what the late Barrett Wendell of Harvard in a much-quoted Chicago address in 1908 called "the privileged class." He is a notable proof of our deep indebtedness to persons of wealth who have consecrated their ample means to Christ and His church as well as the larger good of humanity. It is to them that we owe the substantial gifts which have furthered so immeasurably the progress of the church's work at home and abroad. It is to them that credit is due for the generous endowments which have lengthened the chords and strengthened the stakes of many churches in the changing areas and especially the heart of our great cities. It is to them that we are debtors for the rare and costly art treasures, the impressive and permanent memorials in marble and wood and alabaster, mosaics and pulpit furniture and stained glass windows and pipe organs, which enhance our houses of worship. It is to them that we are indebted for their benefactions to schools and colleges, scientific research and hospitals, libraries, historical and art museums, and innumerable cultural and humane projects. They have been in circumstances enabling them to provide hospitality on a large scale to servants of the Master, which could not otherwise be realized.

Despite his prestige, the goodman of the house was a quiet, reserved follower of Jesus. His very interest in our Lord and His cause may have been a distinct surprise to some of the most intimate disciples. He cherished within his heart a love for Jesus, which he never revealed to the outside world. Speaking at the memorial service for Dr. John DeWitt, long professor of church history at Princeton Theological Seminary, his younger colleague and successor on the faculty, Dr. Frederick W. Loetscher, remarked of the urbane and stately divine, who was a lineal descendant of the founder of Pennsylvania's capital city: "Dr. DeWitt talked little even in his old age about his religious states and said little at any time about personal religion. But in a real sense his Christianity was co-extensive with his life, enveloping it like a sun: and, like these two influences in the natural world, bringing forth and maturing an abundant and beautiful fruitage."

In his delightful volume, *The Soul of England,* the late Dean Inge speaks of the taciturnity of his fellow countrymen and their stoicism in pain and trouble. He tells how Walter Hines Page, the American ambassador to England during World War I, was greatly impressed by the dignity and self-restraint shown by English mourners of both sexes, who repressed all external signs of grief which they were feeling. Page reported how he had been informed that the English soldier dies silently in the hospital "as if he had a secret with his Maker."

The religious attitude of the goodman of the house, especially with respect to Jesus, may not have been ebullient or demonstrative but it was earnest, thoughtful, and profound. His innate reserve made him averse to exposing his soul to the multitude. Here was a man who was not desirous of recognition in the circle of Christ's servants. He was not numbered among the twelve disciples. He did not aspire to a position of honor. He was not present in his own home when the Passover was celebrated and the Lord's Supper was instituted. He was not reluctant to recede gracefully into the background. He desired no theatre for his ego. He had mastered a fine art often missing.

Above all else, his principal desire was to be of some usefulness to the Master. He gave Him the choicest room in the house. His was no nominal token of service to Christ. He gave of his best to the Master. One, whose health had been impaired by severe war experience early in his dedicated career, said to me, "I would like to do something for Jesus Christ." One of the inspirations which should be desired is the resolve to perform some act of loving service for Him who gave us His dying love.

The goodman of the house received his rewards. He placed his home at the service of Christ. Thereafter it was forever enriched and hallowed. It was in that home that the New Testament church had its inception. There is a reference in St. Paul's First Epistle to the Corinthians to "the church that is in the house of Aquila and Priscilla." Some of our present churches held their earliest services in private homes. In tracing the history of my former church in the city of Niagara Falls, New York, I discovered that the initial services were conducted in the residence of one of the charter members. In some small Pennsylvania communities on a Sunday afternoon, one hears the rhythmic clatter of horses' hoofs as large companies of Amish families make their way through the village streets, going from their farms on one side of the town to some plain farm home on the opposite side where on that particular Sabbath services of divine worship are to be held. The Amish continue to use their farm houses as places of worship.

After that dark betrayal night, the upper room became a sacred shrine to which the followers of Jesus repaired. It was there in clandestine fashion for fear of their supposedly powerful enemies that the friends of Jesus waited after they had heard the rumors about His resurrection. It was there that the risen Lord came to them, unobstructed by doors and walls, convincing them of the reality of His resurrection and pro-

nouncing upon them the benediction of His peace,
which evermore passeth human knowing. It was there
one week after the resurrection that the first observance of the first day of the week as the Lord's Day
transpired, while Christ Himself stood in the midst,
emphasizing to His disciples that He continued to have
a body as He had prior to the crucifixion and affording
such proof that it was He who was dead and was alive
again as to evoke the ecstatic and enraptured ex-
clamation of Thomas, "My Lord and my God." It
was there that the faithful, Mary, the mother of Jesus,
among them, waited in prayer for ten quiet days
after He had been received up into glory and until
the wondrous signs of Pentecost betokened the descent
of the Holy Spirit upon the church. The upper room
and entire house was sanctified because Christ was
once received there with honor and love.

There was a home long ago, described in one of
the most beautiful stories of the Old Testament, where
a Shunammite woman set apart an upper chamber
for the saintly prophet, Elisha, whom she described as
a "holy man of God, who passeth by continually."
In a day of tragedy, the prophet came to that room and
there restored to life the young son of the Shunammite
woman and her husband, the owner of a vast farm.

In downtown Philadelphia there stands the mansion
of a once-renowned journalist. The house was ren-
dered famous because of some of the guests entertained
there, General U. S. Grant and Herbert Spencer, the
English social philosopher, among them. Stopping
once at a gasoline station in the colonial spa town of

Berkeley Springs, West Virginia, I was told that in the bay window room of an adjoining house, Washington Irving wrote much of his biography of George Washington, who had often come at an earlier time to the mineral baths at that place. In Germantown, Philadelphia, is the Morris House, acquired not long since by the Federal government as a museum. The building was made of historic significance because Washington and his associates took refuge there while the yellow fever epidemic raged in the city and in that dwelling was transacted for a period of many weeks the business of the then young government.

The Holy Spirit of Christ inhabits the bodies of those who by faith receive Christ as their Saviour. The Apostle Paul impresses upon us the fact that the body is a temple to be kept pure and inviolate from sin. The soul which has known the blessed presence of Christ can never again be regarded as aught but sacred. We who have received Christ by faith are to remember that Christ's sanctifying presence imposes upon us the obligation to guard our souls and bodies against all defilement.

The goodman of the house received a second reward. He will always be known as a friend of the Lord Jesus. An English nobleman requested that he be remembered simply as the friend of Charles James Fox, the statesman and orator. Dickens in *Great Expectations* has Pip visit his old benefactor, Magwitch, the dying ex-convict, who in touching fashion expressed his thankfulness that the boy had never deserted him and, in particular, that he had shown that friendship with more fervor when he was under a dark cloud than when the sun shone.

The goodman of the house befriended Jesus when the opposition of His enemies was at its height and on that night when He was doomed to know the eager rage of every foe.

We have come to this table bearing the high distinction that we are the friends of the Lord Jesus. "Ye are my friends, if ye do whatsoever I command you." "Henceforth I call you not servants . . . but . . . friends." It is here that we realize what a friend we have in Jesus, who will never desert us in the darkest hours. "Greater love hath no man than this, that a man lay down his life for his friends," He says of His perfect sacrifice at Calvary. Let us find our chief honor in being known as friends of the Lord Jesus. Let us count it all joy when we are called upon to confess that friendship in a world where many still view Him with scornful unbelief and are sharply antagonistic to His way of life and salvation. Let us be His friends, when men frown upon His ethical precepts as did the French premier, Clemenceau, who in bitter vindictiveness at the moment President Woodrow Wilson urged greater gentleness and magnanimity towards the vanquished nations, remonstrated, saying, "You talk too much like Jesus Christ." Let us not be ashamed to be recognized as friends of the gospel of the Christ who is the God-man, than whom there was no other good enough to pay the price of sin and no other name in whom is the hope of acceptance with God. Though a skeptical world looks with disdain, that gospel is as St. Paul testified, "the power of God unto salvation to everyone that believeth." Let us strengthen the bonds of that sacred and eternal friendship.

4

Jesus and the Police

"As soon then as he (Jesus) had said unto them, I am he, they went backward, and fell to the ground." JOHN 18:6

It was at the gate of Gethsemane. The temple police, re-enforced by the soldiers from the Roman fort of Antonia, the priests, the avowed enemies of Jesus, the rabble, and Judas the betrayer as their mentor, had come to arrest Jesus. They were astonished to find Jesus Himself drawing near. They were more startled as He inquired, "Whom seek ye?" They replied to His question, "Jesus of Nazareth." With surpassing calmness and overwhelming straightforwardness, He answered, "I am he." They felt awed, shamed, and insecure before Him. The white light of His purity brought a sense of guilt to their souls. They went backward and fell to the ground. Jesus had to recall them to the purpose of their encounter. They had expected to trap Him, whereas He had trapped them.

In the seventh chapter of St. John's Gospel, there is the record of certain officials being dispatched to investigate Jesus. When they listened to Him as He preached, they desisted from placing Him under arrest. Returning without their prisoner they reported, "Never man spake like this man." No man had dared to lay hands upon Him.

What was so awe inspiring in the figure and personality of Jesus that dark betrayal night? What filled the temple police and the soldiers with such awe?

Many individuals have been known to be well-nigh overpowering in their impressiveness.

After Moses descended the slopes of Sinai, where he held high communion with God and received the tables of the law, it is said that "he wist not that his face shone." An unearthly lustre begotten of his meeting with the Most High suffused his countenance.

Stephen, the first Christian martyr, whose eagle eye could pierce beyond the grave and who went to his frightful death breathing out the grace of forgiveness for his cruel foes, became radiant in those last, terrible moments. The bystanders "saw his face as though it were the face of an angel."

In Roman history there is the tale of the Gaulish slave who had been sent by Scylla to conduct Marius to his execution. At the sight of the slave advancing to the door of his cell, Marius, who was possessed of an august presence, exclaimed in a voice that seemed capable of shaking the world: "Fellow, darest thou to slay Caius Marius?" The slave threw down his weapon and departed from the prison without his prisoner.

Preaching in Boston not long since, I requested my taxi driver to take me to historic Charlestown. There I thought of a Puritan ancestor who settled in that place in 1630 and who was a charter member of Charlestown's ancient First Congregational Church. I saw the mast of Old Ironsides, one of America's most famous vessels once preserved from destruction by a young medical college professor's moving poem. Towering over the area was the Bunker Hill monument at the scene of the Revolutionary War battle. I recalled how after his masterful oration at the laying of the cornerstone of that great shaft, those who saw Daniel Webster observed an indescribably grand expression on his countenance. Someone who saw him remarked, "No one could possibly look that grand."

Sidney Smith, the English wit and man of letters said that Francis Horner had the Ten Commandments inscribed on his face.

Dean Robert K. Root in recalling his interview with Woodrow Wilson, then President of Princeton University, as he, a fledgling in the academic realm, presented himself as a candidate for a preceptorship, said: "Before five minutes had passed I knew that I was in the presence of a very great man. I did recognize that I had never before talked face to face with so compelling a person" (article on Woodrow Wilson by Charles G. Osgood in *The Lives of Eighteen from Princeton*, Princeton University Press, 1946).

What was there about the mien and face of Jesus that so profoundly impressed and overwhelmed His enemies and the temple police?

There was the grandeur of His absolute innocence. A man burdened with the consciousness of guilt might have searched for a place of refuge among the recesses of the garden. Even a guiltless man might have refrained from coming out with boldness to face his foes. Jesus had a unique and unparalleled innocence. Pilate perceived that sinlessness and declared Him to be without defect. Indeed it was essential that Jesus shoud be "holy, harmless, undefiled, separate from sinners," if He were to bear our condemnation for our sins upon the cross. Perfect manhood as much as true Godhood was required if the sacrifice of Calvary were to be perfect and acceptable.

While none of us know the complete freedom from any taint of evil that pertained to Jesus, there is a relative innocence which we do well to covet.

Vicious blackmail artists threatened to besmirch the reputation of the mighty London preacher, Charles

Haddon Spurgeon. Spurgeon, undaunted, defied them to emblazon all that they knew about his record across the skies.

John B. Gough, the convert from drunkenness who became America's best-known apostle of abstinence, collapsed while lecturing in the pulpit of the Frankford Presbyterian Church of Philadelphia. He died hours later in the residence of a physician two doors from that edifice. Before he fell to the floor in that sudden and mortal attack, Gough uttered the ringing injunction: "Young man, keep your record clean!"

Standing before a hostile ruler, the Apostle Paul proudly testified: "I have exercised myself always to have a conscience void of offense towards God and man."

What a shield of protection and courage is borne by those who have the testimony of a good conscience and the invaluable asset of transparent, irreproachable character!

The temple police were impressed deeply by Christ's absolute candor concerning His identity. It was to the woman of Samaria, who referred to the Messiah, that Jesus disclosed Himself, saying, "I that speak unto thee am he." We as Christians should never be timid about confessing the true nature of Jesus to the world, pronouncing Him unequivocably as the Son of God, the God-man, the Saviour of the world, rather than resorting to such vague, nebulous, poetic appelations as The Man of Nazareth, the Stranger of Galilee, the Man Nobody Knows. I recall a veteran of the Presbyterian ministry, who declined to offer prayer at exercises in a public high school when it was stipulated that he should delete from his prayer any use of the Name which is above every name. We should never be ashamed to honor openly the name and above all, the eternal power and Godhead as well as the Saviourhood of the Lord Jesus.

More than the innocence and candor of Jesus, it was the supernatural glory of His presence that awed the police and soldiers and His rabid enemies. Trailing clouds of glory, the aura of the eternal world in which he reigned ere worlds began, and the light that never was on sea or land struck the posse speechless. That light ineffable, that far-beaming blaze of majesty which belonged to Him when He sat, as Milton suggests, in the midst of Trinal Unity at heaven's high council table was manifest at certain moments of His earthly ministry, though he was clad in a simple homespun garb of a peasant.

Peter sensed the celestial wonder as well as the sinlessness of Jesus, when in a boat on Galilee he protested, "Depart from me, O Lord, for I am a sinful man."

Making the journey to Jerusalem for the last time, one who witnessed Jesus steadfastly setting His face in the direction of the cross, wrote, "Jesus went before them: and they were amazed; and as they followed, they were afraid."

There must have been that which was extraordinarily subduing in the voice and aspect of Jesus in the closing hours of the first Palm Sunday when with a scourge of cords in His hand and tremendous force in His personality, He caused the money changers, who made His Father's house a den of thieves to take flight in terror from the precincts of the temple which they had desecrated by their exploitation.

On the Mount of Transfiguration, while He was praying, the fashion of His countenance was altered and His whole being seemed arrayed with the brilliance of the heavenly places.

Immediately after the resurrection there was something stunning and electrifying about the presence of Christ and the angelic beings who were in attendance at the event. It is strange, is it not, that some Biblical interpreters have overlooked the otherworldly appearance of Christ at that climactic time and continue to anticipate His establishing a mundane regime while manifesting Himself in a fleshly, materialistic fashion, altogether wanting in that rarefied aspect which was so pronounced when He showed Himself alive after His passion.

On the Damascene road, Saul of Tarsus was arrested by a flashing light and a searching voice, compelling him to fall to the ground: "Saul, Saul, why persecutest thou me?" There was a lofty majesty in that face, a starry radiance in those eyes, a supernal note of authority betokening a deity nigh in that voice.

On the isle of Patmos, where he was held in lonely captivity for the testimony of Jesus, John envisaged the glorified Christ. His head and hairs were white

like wool, as white as snow, and His eyes were as a
flame of fire and His feet were like unto fine brass,
as if they were burned in a furnace, and His voice was
as the sound of many waters. When John saw Jesus, on
whose bosom he had leaned in the upper room but
who now irradiated the splendors of the New Jerusalem, he fell at his feet as dead.

In the same apocalyptic book of the New Testament, John relates how the ages will attain their consummation with two prayer meetings. One prayer meeting will consist of those enraptured members of re-
deemed society who will be lost in adoration of the
Lamb of God slain for sins. The other group will
consist of those who confined themselves to the natural
and ignored and denied the supernatural and who,
confronted by the majesty of Christ, will implore the
rocks and mountains to fall upon them and hide them
from the awesome presence of the eternal Christ.

The involuntary obeisance of His enemies which
came at the gate of the garden and in the flickering
torchlight, presaged the homage which has been accorded Jesus through the centuries even by an un-
believing world declining to acknowledge Him as God.
There are four figures in the date borne by today's
newspapers. They epitomize the world's awe-filled acknowledgment of Jesus. Officially we date our docu-
ments, "In the year of our Lord." All history has been
divided by the periods designated "Before Christ" and
"In the year of our Lord."

There is the obeisance which has been paid to Christ

by His severest critics, who have mingled tributes of praise and appreciation with their denials, doubts, and disparagements.

Ernest Renan in the conclusion of his eloquent but skeptical life of Jesus declared that whatever might be the surprises of the future, Jesus' worship would grow young without ceasing and His legend would call forth tears without end.

David Friedrich Strauss, the German rationalist whose pioneering effort at a life of Jesus caused George Eliot, the translator, to suffer the loss of her faith, admitted that Jesus is the highest symbol of religion within the reach of our thought and the greatest religious genius in history.

There is the enforced obeisance which will be given to Jesus ultimately by His enemies. In the Epistle to the Philippians, St. Paul, after speaking of the incarnation and humiliation of Jesus, looks prophetically to the day when at the name of Jesus every knee shall bow, of things in heaven and things in earth, and things under the earth, and that every tongue shall confess that Jesus Christ is Lord, to the glory of God the Father. In a previous Epistle, II Thessalonians, and with more lurid phrases, Paul dips into the future beyond what human eye can see, to that juncture "when the Lord Jesus shall be revealed from heaven with His mighty angels, in flaming fire taking vengeance on them that know not God, and that obey not the gospel of our Lord Jesus Christ." If, in the course of His first advent with its great humility, Jesus struck men with awe, how overwhelming must be the majesty of His return and the inconceivable brightness of His coming in glory!

It is not enough that we be filled with reverential awe as we stand in the presence of Christ. He invites us to draw near in faith and love and find Him our Saviour from sin and death, our loving Friend and elder Brother. There, in the love that casts out fear, reverence will continue, but dread will vanish. Great joy and peace will fill our hearts as with the eyes of faith we behold Him, if but faintly, with the darkling veil between, ever waiting for that day when His glory shall be seen by those who love His appearing.

5

The Real Villain behind the Cross

"And led him (Jesus) away to Annas first; for he was father-in-law to Caiaphas, which was the high priest that same year." JOHN 18:13

Annas, according to Dr. Charles Anderson Scott,* the eminent British scholar, was probably the chief instigator of the plot against Jesus, which eventuated in the cross.

*See article on Annas in Hasting's *Dictionary of Christ and the Gospels.*

Despite the meager attention accorded Annas as the principal culprit in the conspiracy against Jesus, it was the preliminary examination before the former high priest that initiated the succession of illegal trials which was climaxed by the crucifixion.

For Jesus to be tried before Annas was comparable to a New York political and social reformer being subjected to trial before the officials of Tammany Hall. There was no legal warrant for the trial before Annas. Annas sent Jesus, bound and in the ignominious capacity of a prisoner, to his son-in-law, the reigning high priest, Caiaphas. Caiaphas questioned Jesus while the Jewish supreme court, the Sanhedrin, was assembling for its illicit night session. Caiaphas had unwittingly enunciated the principle underlying the substitutionary atonement which Jesus made by His death. He had said: "It is expedient for you that one man should die for the people, and that the whole nation should perish not." Jesus confounded Caiaphas by His silence. Then, in the most stupendous of all the stupendous moments of our Saviour's earthly life. He was compelled to meet the supreme issue of His deity. Caiaphas administered the Jewish oath, saying, "I adjure thee by the living God, that thou tell us whether thou be the Christ, the Son of God." Jesus boldly affirmed, "Thou hast said." Previously when some sought to take Jesus by force and make Him a king, He refused. When the disciples were eager to herald Him as the Messiah, He checked their fervor. Now in the presence of His antagonists and of the Jewish elders and in the final hour of His ministry. He made an unconditional avowal of His deity. As a consequence the chief priests rent their robes and shrieked that He was guilty of blasphemy. They condemned Him as guilty of death. The Sanhedrin did not possess the power of imposing a sentence of execution. It was necessary to send Jesus to Pilate, who represented the civil authority. Meanwhile, the Sanhedrin assembled after dawn to legalize the action which they had taken concerning Jesus. Their attempt at legalizing their condemnation of Jesus is a demonstration of the fact that one can be thoroughly legal and at the same time utterly wrong from the moral standpoint.

Pilate refused the demand of the Sanhedrin that Jesus should be put to death. He insisted on conducting his own questioning. He extracted from Jesus the significant admission that He was a king. He reached the verdict, which the ages have re-echoed, that no fault could be found in Jesus. In a gesture fraught with political strategy, Pilate sent Jesus to Herod, half Idumean, half Samaritan, and tetrarch of Galilee. Pilate and Herod had been at variance and by this overture of appeasement Pilate "made friends" with Herod. Puzzled by Jesus' reticence before his curious questions, Herod refused to exercise jurisdiction over Jesus, the Man of Galilee, and returned Him to the Roman procurator. Pilate yielded at last to the popular clamor, when the mob chose Barabbas in preference to Jesus as the prisoner to be freed. With grave misgivings, he pronounced judicial sentence. Thus numbered with the transgressors, Jesus was led to the brutal and disgraceful death of a criminal.

Behind the trials and plots and popular clamor which found their consummation in the cross was the man most responsible for history's blackest crime, Annas, the father-in-law of Caiaphas.

Annas was an Alexandrian Jew who was appointed high priest by Quirinius about the year A.D. 6. Luke in his Gospel refers to the fact that John the Baptist began his ministry when Annas was high priest. Annas was deposed from his lofty sacerdotal office by Pontius Pilate's predecessor, Valerius Gratus, in about the year A.D. 15. Each of the five sons of Annas and his son-in-law, Joseph Caiaphas, served in the role of high priest. Although he had not officiated in his office of high priest for many years, Annas was at the time of the public ministry of Jesus the most dominant and influential personage in Hebrew religious circles. The late Dr. Maitland Alexander, of Pittsburgh, once called Annas "the numismatical agent of the Jewish politics of his day." Annas was a frustrated ecclesiastical politician, always the most degraded variety of religionist. He was a Sadducee. He was a leader in the most fashionable and powerful church of the time. The Sadducees were the haughty, wealthy, worldly, aristocratic church of their age. In that wing of Jewry, Annas was the champion "wire puller." Secular historians report that he had loaned money to influential Romans to such an extent that he could blackmail them to do anything he wanted. As the principal Sadducee, Annas, more than any other, typified the socially prominent, rationalistic, ritualistic form of religion which controlled the temple in Jerusalem and there offered the emasculated creed, denying immortality, the resurrection of the body, the existence of angels, and most of the spiritual and supernatural elements of the Old Testament. After the year A.D. 70, when the armies of the Roman emperor, Titus, destroyed Jerusalem, leaving not one stone upon another in the temple, the Sadducees became extinct. Their more devout, believing, and orthodox contemporaries, the Pharisees, despite their legalism and literalism and pedantry as well as their ironclad creed, survived in pattern and spirit. Their emphasis on teaching and preaching rather than liturgy persisted and continues to prevail in modern Judaism.

Annas was the power behind the priestly throne of his son-in-law, Caiaphas. Rostand in his drama, *Cyrano de Bergerac,* makes the comic, tragic de Bergerac the controlling force behind the life and romance of Christian and Roxanne. Cardinal Richelieu, as a so-called prince of the church, virtually governed France in the regime of Louis XIII and precipitated the Thirty Years War, primarily by virtue of his hostility to Austria. In the reign of Elizabeth I, England's policies were dictated largely by William Cecil, Lord Burghley, who was the father-in-law of Edward DeVere, Earl of Oxford, to whom some critics have been disposed to attribute the plays generally ascribed to Shakespeare. Churchill in his recent history speaks of Burghley as the foremost statesman of sixteenth century England and remarks about his immense industry and consuming thirst for knowledge of the affairs of the realm. The major voice behind the throne of Mary

Queen of Scots was the Italian basso and musician, David Rizzio, who was at length assassinated in a plot in which Lord Darnley, whose marriage with Queen Mary, Rizzio had engineered, was a leading participant. Until his assassination on the last day of the year 1916, that diabolical figure, the Russian monk, Rasputin, known by his sobriquet, the holy devil, had gained the ascendancy over the ill-fated czar and cza-rina. As in the case of Annas, the power behind the throne is often far greater than the incumbent.

In his interview with Jesus, Annas was met with silence. What reciprocity could there be between Annas and Jesus? St. Paul's assertion that the natural man discerneth not the things of the Spirit of God is sufficient explanation of the inability of Annas to comprehend Jesus. Apply Christ's Beatitudes to the life of Annas and you will perceive at once that he could enter into no real understanding of the mystery of the Master. Think of Annas in the light of those pronouncements: "Blessed are the pure in heart: for they shall see God." "Blessed are the poor in spirit: for theirs is the kingdom of heaven." "Blessed are they that hunger and thirst after righteousness: for they shall be filled." Those who declare that they go from church service to church service and sermon to sermon and find no message for their souls should study themselves in the light of St. Paul's pronouncement on the dullness of the unregenerate heart and the explicit teachings of the Beatitudes of Jesus.

The one statement Jesus made to Annas ought to make us pensive. Some have found in His words a repudiation of the penchant for a cult of arcanum, the esoteric, and the ritual of secrecy. He said: "I spake openly to the world; I even taught in the synagogue, and in the temple whither the Jews always resort; and in secret have I said nothing." Then as if speaking not only to Annas but to those of all ages who wonder about Him, He said: "Why askest thou me? Ask them which heard me, what I have said unto them. Behold, they know what I said." If one is puzzled about Jesus, he should make a candid review of His life and work in the world and the effects which He produced on society and in the lives of His followers. Annas was infuriated at the close of his interview with Jesus. One of the officers in attendance smote the Master, who made no obeisance and gave no sign of intimidation before the one-time high priest.

Annas, astute hierarch that he was, was primarily a religious exploiter and racketeer. He utilized religion to promote his selfish interests. He had accumulated a fortune by levying temple taxes on the people. It was he who, more than any other, engineered the sale of sheep and doves for sacrifice in the temple courts. He and his colleagues maintained large country estates where animals were bred for sale to temple worshippers. He had started what was known as the bazaar of Annas.

What crimes have been committed in the name of religion by those who have used the church and the cult to advance their own financial and political interests! What evil has been wrought under the guise of religion! There have been the inquisitions, the Spanish

Inquisition being one of the more celebrated. There has been bigotry and intolerance and malignity of spirit. One remembers the burning of persons accused of witchcraft, the suppression of scientific truth and literature in the name of a religious protectorate of the people, the obscurantism which has placed a premium on ignorance and mediocrity and opposed scholarship. One thinks of those who opposed anesthesia on religious grounds and those who defended human slavery on the basis of Bible texts. Today we have the menace of bingo sponsored by certain churches. Beware of those marching under the banner of religion to accomplish evil.

Annas resented the fact that Jesus interfered with his life, his morality, his business and vested interests.

Amaziah, the priest, warned Jeroboam II of the dangerous prophet Amos, who was inveighing against his established and profitable order of religious corruption at the shrine city of Bethel.

The Gadarene meat packers became irate and alarmed when the pork business was imperiled by Jesus who, in performing a miracle of mercy, drove the unclean and demonic spirits out of the tormented man and sent them into the swine that immediately became wild and plunged furiously over a cliff into the sea. They told Jesus "to get going" out of their country.

Through the preaching of Paul and Silas there was converted a young woman who had been exploited as a soothsayeer and one possessed of a spirit of divination at Philippi. Her exploiting masters, who had capitalized on her abnormality were so angered that they started an intense opposition determined to banish Paul and Silas from the city.

The Temple of Diana at Ephesus contained many architectural features that were reproduced in our own country during the classic revival of the last century. The preaching of St. Paul in the city of Ephesus had turned many from idols to the living God. The city was filled with silversmiths who gained a livelihood from fashioning little silver shrines and idols. Demetrius, the silversmith, rallied his fellow craftsmen and warned of the damage the Apostle Paul's preaching was working in their business: "Sirs, ye know that by this craft we have our wealth." In their very insecurity, the jewelers of Ephesus became insistent and created a mighty uproar as they shouted, "Great is Diana of the Ephesians." No small stir was created as they resolved to expel the apostle from their city because he menaced their trade.

In 1789 there were English business interests that opposed violently the Christian missionary venture of William Carey as he went out to India. They recognized that some of their activities could not be reconciled with the Christian gospel.

Christ and Christianity are most bitterly opposed by those who resent any intrusion into their conduct and business and social relationships. Much that is disguised as intellectual doubt is a camouflage of a person's distaste for the revolutionizing force that the spirit of Christ introduces into his moral life. "We will not have this man reign over us," is their vehement protest against Christ's claim to lordship over their lives.

Like Annas, we have our little day of sitting in judgment on Christ. We can dismiss Him, ignoring the fact that He wears the royal diadem of His Father's throne. We can receive and honor Him as our Saviour and our Master, remembering that day when we will be summoned to appear before His judgment seat to give an account of the deeds done in the body.

6

A Tale of Two Maids

"Now Peter sat without in the palace: and a damsel came unto him, saying, Thou also wast with Jesus of Galilee." MATTHEW 26:69

In the accounts of Peter's denial of his Lord, Matthew and Mark mention two maids. Luke and John refer to one maid. John specifies that the maid-servant in question kept the door.

These women sought to bask in the light of the prestige of their employer, the high priest, Caiaphas. They exceeded their prerogatives as servants in the house of Caiaphas by their attitude towards Peter. Their pride in their position as servants of the highest ecclesiastical dignitary reached a state of amusing if not annoying arrogance.

In the brief months of his tenure, President Garfield had a coachman who felt that the unpretentious structure of the Vermont Avenue Disciples Church, in Washington, where Garfield attended and had sometimes preached, did not befit the chief executive of our nation. Hence the officious coachman drove the president to the Vermont Avenue Church, left him there and drove to the street in front of a more imposing church and there parked the presidential carriage until the accustomed time of the dismissal of the Vermont Avenue Disciples congregation drew near and then returned to convey the president to the White House.

It was a servant in the household of the Eastern Orthodox metropolitan in Jerusalem, who turned away from his employer's door the Arabs who were fulfilling their engagement to bring the priceless Dead Sea scrolls. Their uncouth appearance had led the servant, unaware of their appointment, to turn them from the threshold. An unknown servant might have caused the loss of the recently unearthed scrolls to the scholarly world.

The maids in the residence of Caiaphas assumed that their position in so prominent an household invested them with an authority which they did not actually possess. There have been many who have been thrust into places of power for which they seem devoid of personal worthiness. I think of college presidents, who have been surely a far cry from their illustrious predecessors who brought the lustre of their intellectuality and scholarship to the office. I think of clergymen in historic pulpits, who obviously lack the qualifications of erudition and eloquence possessed by the distinguished and saintly men who preceded them. I think of executives of influential firms whose moral standards have been far from commensurate with the gifts of influence and responsibility with which they have been entrusted. I think of scions of famous families, who were largely descended from the high place of culture and character attained by their antecedents. Rabbi Stephen S. Wise told of a man he met when they were fellow volunteers laboring in a shipyard during the First World War. The man boasted of his descent from one of the signers of the Declaration of Independence. The famous rabbi was minded to inform the man that he would never suspect his notable inheritance. I think of heads of nations, governors of states, mayors of great cities, judges in the courts, wearing the official mantles of earlier figures, who were the luminaries of their generation. The latter day incumbents fell tragically short of the respect won by earlier occupants for their lofty posts.

It is not identification with an outstanding position, name, or institution that merits honor but the gifts and graces of mind and heart which one brings to and demonstrates in the place.

The maids in Caiaphas' household transgressed the limits of their rightful province as servants in the house when they sought to taunt Simon Peter. They were impudent, impertinent prattlers. Everyone has his proper sphere and no little sound judgment is required to prevent him from usurping privileges not belonging to him. On occasions when we are disposed to speak and act, when it ill becomes us so to do, we should remind ourselves of the admonition of St. Paul in one of the earliest New Testament books, "Study to be quiet, and to do your own business." It was commented editorially of a certain jurist and historical scholar at his demise that he minded his own business and let the rest of the world go by. The maids of the house of Caiaphas suffered from an uninhibited "interferiority" complex. We need to pray for the grace of minding our own business."

These women were guilty of the sin of trying to embarrass another person. They derived sinister gratification from taunting, mortifying, and intimidating Simon Peter. Such boorishness still exists. Ill-bred persons attempt to belittle others in their presence, expose their lack of refinement or education, their blunders of times past, their personal idiosyncrasies and deficiences, conjuring up "old, unhappy far-off things and battles long ago." In his *Idea of a University,* Cardinal Newman cites the generally accepted definition of a gentleman as one who never inflicts pain. There is the so-called practical joker, playing his pranks at the expense and with the attempted depreciation of others, thereby divulging quite unwittingly his own emotional immaturity and sense of insecurity, while making his ludicrous and futile effort to establish his supposed superiority. It is in that category that the maids, who sought to put Peter to shame, can be located psychologically. It is the Golden Rule which constrains us to exercise respect for the sensibilities of others, acting towards them as we would have them demean themselves with respect to us.

Here were women who evoked the worst phases of Peter's nature. They elicited his disloyalty to his Master in the hour of trial, his emotional instability, his dastardly fears, his old and largely overcome habit of profanity. We ought always to search our hearts as to whether we call forth the nobler or the baser elements of the nature in those whose lives we touch. Dr. Samuel Johnson said of Edmund Burke: "That man calls forth all my powers."

In the opening years of our century two popular dramas described somewhat mysterious characters who had the capacity to awaken within others a desire to express their nobler selves. Charles Rand Kennedy in *The Servant in the House* wrote of a missionary bishop who came incognito into the vicarage of a materialistic, English clergyman and by his spirit of Christlikeness transformed the lives of the members of that household, recalling them from self-centered ambitions to unselfish devotion to the service of others. Jerome K. Jerome in *The Passing of the Third Floor Back* delineated a similar pattern in an English boarding house, where a mysterious person, who took up lodging in the humble third floor back room, awakened within each of his fellow boarders a desire to live nobly and on a loftier moral plane than they had known.

The maidservants of Caiaphas were the agents who led Peter to deny his Lord. They were by no means the last instruments in the hand of the Evil One to urge men and women to infidelity to their Lord. Sometimes professors in our educational institutions and writers, whose works have had much currency among students, have invited young men and women to abandon their faith in the supernatural Christ and the supernatural Bible.

In 1849, the Rev. Elisha Fiske, a New England Congregational minister observing the fiftieth anniversary of ordination delivered a sermon which lasted two hours. Standing in his pulpit in Wrentham, Massachusetts, this man, who at the early age of five had read through the Bible, and said that he owed his religious convictions to his mother and a village minister, issued a warning to his congregation. He seemed aware that a tidal wave of doubt concerning the Bible would soon engulf even the churches, although few had then sensed its imminence. He told his hearers: "Take care of the Bible and see that its sacred contents be not theorized away, and their hold weakened on the hearts and consciences of men." Alas, ministers in the pulpit have by their denegations of the truth of the Bible and the fundamental articles of our mysterious creed caused their hearers to minimize and disavow faith in the mighty acts whereby Christ has won for us life and immortality, concentrating their at-

tention exclusively on the humanity of Jesus. There
are those who create a social atmosphere altogether
alien to Christian ideals and conduct. The professor
of religion in a well-known school of engineering once
told me about a little coterie of men degraded in
thought and devoid of Christian standards and outlook, who foregathered nightly about a general store in
a Hoosier village and tended to blast the faith and
blight the personality of every young man who ven-
tured into their irreligious and obscene fellowship.
Supposed friends, often laying great claims to social
prowess, have tempted others to belie their Master as
they have bidden them to social engagements which
included no consideration of the sanctity of the Lord's
Day and the conventional hours and higher claims of
Christian worship. They have allured professing Christians to social customs which altogether repudiated the
principles of the New Testament. It behooves us as
Christians to be vigilant lest at any time we should
entice another person into an attitude or act not con-
sonant with his commitment to Christ as the Lord
of his life.

There is a phrase in the Presbyterian marriage ceremony, prepared largely by Dr. Henry Van Dyke, and
which is applicable to other contacts in life: "As Thou
in Thy Providence hast brought them together." We
usually think of those who will be brought into touch
with us as "ships that pass in the night" or who will
be introduced into our lives to turn us to righteousness
and bless us. There are other encounters which we
must have with those who have it within their power

to accomplish our undoing, lead us into temptation, and leave us sullied. There are strange meetings with someone who implanted religious doubts in your mind or led you to abandon, if only for a moment, your Christian ideals. There are persons whom we may well regret having met even as Peter must have despised the moment when these hudibrastic young women appeared on the horizon of his career.

Peter had made himself particularly liable to moral danger by the spiritual location in which he placed himself. He followed Jesus afar off. He moved in the circle of the enemies of Christ and the idly curious. He warmed himself by the charcoal fire in the palace courtyard belonging to Jesus' bitterest foes. He had come "to see the end," motivated more by curiosity than by conscience. He allowed himself to be ranged with his Lord's enemies. He was standing in the way of sinners and sitting in the seat of the scornful. In Matthew Henry's quaint descriptive phrase, he was "loath to be seen on the side of despised godliness." He offered no protests to the jests and ridicule to which the name of Jesus was being subjected. He may have feigned a laugh in order that he might be numbered among them. Many follow Christ afar off because their aim is to be conformed to this world, while according Him nominal homage.

There are those who crave social popularity and acceptance at the risk of the compromise of their convictions. Meanwhile they cherish vestigial spiritual aspirations. Some cherish an unchristian habit or alliance or a secret sin that keeps them remote from

Christ. Some are hoping to be safe spiritually while giving meager attention to the ordinances and worship of the church, the Bible, prayer, and Christian activities. It is in such hours that tragedy and danger descend upon the soul. Keep close to the Saviour. Never be abashed to acknowledge your fealty and allegiance to Him. Then the maidservants of Caiaphas and their modern counterparts will have little power to fell you.

7

That Choice Goes by Forever

> *"And so Pilate, willing to content the people, released Barabbas unto them."*
> MARK 15:15

Barabbas has had a peculiar fascination for writers. Christopher Marlowe gave the name Barabbas to his *The Jew of Malta,* a drama that anticipated Shakespeare's *The Merchant of Venice.* Marie Corelli, the once-popular English novelist, produced a novel entitled *Barabbas.* The recent Scandinavian novelist, Pär Lagerkvist, within this decade has given another imaginative work on Barabbas in which he attempts to picture the life of the Biblical character following his release. Lagerkvist fancies Barabbas at the scene of the crucifixion and at the garden sepulchre, has him interview those who knew Jesus personally, and portrays his struggle with doubt. He gives his readers a man too brutal to comprehend the mystery of Christ, the One Altogether Lovely, yet obsessed with Him and His teachings. He delineates a man who is sullen and bewildered, and, in his spiritual confusion, was among those responsible for the conflagration which devastated Rome under Nero, and at length went to death on a cross with other victims of the Neronian persecution, although he was ever at a loss to understand Christ's precept, "Love one another." Further witness of the appeal of Barabbas to the modern literary mind is the dramatic poem of Sara Bard Field, the former suffragette, who portrays Barabbas as a revolutionary.

The name of Barabbas, who was released in response to popular clamor and in the stead of Jesus, would suggest in the Hebrew tongue that he was the son of a rabbi or religious teacher. Adolf Deissman, the Berlin scholar, in his *Mysterium Christi,* hints that Barabbas' first name may have been *Jesus,* hence the opportunity for a kind of play on the names on the the part of Pilate. The first slender volume written by that prolific author of religious and historical volumes, the late Clarence Edward Macartney, was entitled

The Minister's Son and dedicated to the then president of the United States, Woodrow Wilson, a son of the manse. The purpose of the little book was to indicate the large company of men of great influence and distinction who were sons of ministers of the gospel. There have been, unfortunately, sons unworthy of their inheritance, a discredit to their honored fathers, some of whom have led turpitudinous careers as did Barabbas, and others of whom have become the embittered propagandists of cynicism and unbelief. A good, religious family background is not a sure defense against a misspent life and an ignoble end.

Barabbas is characterized in the New Testament as a "notable prisoner." Some prisoners lie deserted and forgotten by their fellowmen, known, as their long sentences are fulfilled, solely to a few prison authorities. Some prisoners attain far greater note than their fellows. There are prisoners for conscience sake. Though chained in prisons dark, they are still in heart and conscience free. In that noble company there were St. Paul, penning his greatest letters from prison; St. John who was held captive amid the salt mines of Patmos, when he wrote his apocalypse of the New Jerusalem and of things to come in the unfolding drama of human history; Boethius, the sixth century Roman senator and philosopher, who within prison walls, where he was sentenced by Theodoric the Goth, produced his classic *Consolations of Philosophy;* John Bunyan in Bedford jail. Some notable prisoners have gained their fame from aspects of their careers other than their incarceration. One remembers Sir Walter

Raleigh, writing his *History of the World* in the tower of London, where he was sent by reason of his opposition to the policy of appeasement towards Spain adopted by James I; Hitler, formulating his *Mein Kampf* while in jail in the year following the end of World War I; Shah Sahan, the builder at Agra in India of the gleaming white marble mausoleum for his favorite wife, the Taj Mahal, spending his final days imprisoned by his son and successor in a room from which he could catch sight by means of an improvised mirror of the world's most resplendent tomb; O. Henry, who within the grim gray walls of Ohio State Penitentiary at Columbus wrote some of his ingenious short stories; Eugene V. Debs, many times candidate for the presidency, confined to Atlanta Penitentiary during our participation in World War I. Other prisoners derive their notoriety from their crimes, which have necessitated their payment of a debt to society.

Barabbas probably did not launch out on his career as a criminal. He was an insurrectionist and champion of the home rule or nationalist party, crusading for emancipation from Palestine's subjugation to the domination of Rome. He belonged to the same vehement political party as did Simon the Zealot, one of Jesus' disciples. His position was comparable to that of the home rule or Sinn Fein group in Ireland. There was in Barabbas in his early years something of the character of that red haired Scot, Rob Roy, celebrated by Sir Walter Scott in one of his novels, and the earlier and shadowy outlaw hero of England, Robin Hood, and his henchmen in Sherwood Forest. Colonial Pennsylvania had the irrepressible Scotch-Irishmen known as the "Paxtang boys." Led by Lazarus Stewart and residing in the region of Harrisburg, these fiery, truculent Presbyterians were aroused to militant action by the depredations wrought in their settlements by hostile Indians. Not only did they desire to prevent further onslaughts from the savages, they were eager for more governmental protection of their homes and such security did not seem forthcoming from a Quaker dominated assembly. They became virtual vigilantes and once marched on the city of Philadelphia where they believed that the Friends were sheltering the guilty Indians. Earlier their Presbyterian pastor had endeavored to dissuade them from violence. At the threshold of Philadelphia, they were mollified by the sagacious action of Benjamin Franklin.

At the outset Barabbas may have been a dreamer. Nurtured by his father in the lore and history of the Hebrew people, he had been fired by patriotic emotion. He contemned Rome more than he feared God. He was a young man of hot blood and turbulent temper. For a time this young, strong, eager man, cherished his dream of leading a victorious and ever-increasing body of Jewish patriots until the Roman yoke would be overthrown and Israelites would again be in the seats of the mighty, which their fathers had occupied. He longed to play a principal role in the dramatic day when the Roman eagle would be pulled down from the castle of Antonias and the banner of Israel there unfurled.

Somehow Barabbas in his zeal became misled and

killed a man in his insurrection activities. No longer a champion, he was ranked with the criminals.

Pilate in his desperate measures to avoid sentencing Jesus to death resorted to the practice of offering to release a prisoner to the people. It was now an issue before the people as to whether they would select Barabbas or Jesus. They clamored for the liberation of the rough desperado, whom they had once lionized, and for the crucifixion of the innocent and holy Jesus.

In the popular choice of Barabbas, whose name, incidentally, appears in all four Gospels, we have an impressive demonstration of the fact that popular preferences are often far from being right. The old Latin saying that the voice of the people is the voice of God was repudiated eternally in Pilate's judgment hall. John Wesley and his intellectually gifted sister were once discussing this very issue. Trying to be conclusive, Wesley said: "The voice of the people is the voice of God." "Yes," replied the sister, "the voice of the people cried, 'Crucify Him, crucify Him.' "

Today's popular heroes will be unrecognized if not ostracized tomorrow. England treated Wellington thus. America accorded Admiral Dewey the same fickle treatment. The best sellers of this year are not likely to be regarded as classics a score of years hence. Superior speakers and writers are more likely to be overlooked by the undiscriminating public while some inferior grade of speaker is received widely and enthusiastically and some superficial author will head the sales lists. The man who captures today's crowds will not hold captive the centuries. A Toronto educator once said in my presence that our aim should not be to be popular but rather respected. Multitudes of Americans are far more interested in bubble gum than in the finer things of life. Popular tastes are at a low level. Who could be so stupid that he would rely on the shallow judgments of the mob?

In a most suggestive essay entitled *Crowds,* the late New England Congregational clergyman, Gerald Stanley Lee, complains that the accentuation of crowds has influenced for evil every realm of our living. Education has been designed entirely for the masses and with no consideration for the exceptional and talented youth. There is a hush of disappointment when only a small audience appears. It spreads like a contagion to the speaker and those present in the room. The value of land is determined by the number of footfalls pasing by in a period of twenty-four hours. Says Dr. Lee: "Modern man has a crowd soul, a crowd creed. It takes ten thousand men to make him think" (*Crowds* by Gerald Stanley Lee, Doubleday, Page and Co., 1913). "The church of our forefathers, founded on personality is exchanged for the church of democracy, founded on crowds and getting the most people. The inevitable result of such thinking, the crowd clergyman is seen on every hand among us — the agent of an audience, who, instead of telling an audience what they ought to do, runs errands for them morning, noon, and night." It was in opposition to the church and the clergy giving the people what they demand rather than what they need that our Saviour sounded His warning: "Woe unto you when all men speak well of you." The gravest error of churches and clergy is that of falling into the disposition of Pilate, namely, that of "wishing to content the multitude."

The voice of the people can seldom be accepted as the voice of God, hence, the voice of truth and right. The choice of the multitude in Pilate's tribunal that early morning shows the world's fallacious standards of success. Barabbas, the dreamer who eventuated in the desparado, was considered by many to be the successful man, the recipient of popular acclaim and freedom. Jesus seemed the tragic failure. Though that scaffold to which they condemned Him now sways the future, He seemed a pathetic soul who had lost His hold on the multitudes, was no longer able to win their votes, and at thirty-three was being hastened to His death with a diminishing band of followers, receding increasingly into the sheltering shadows for fear of His enemies.

The plaudits of the crowd and the momentary conquest of their fluctuating affections, escape from adversity and disappointment, a place of prestige gained by political maneuvering, constitute what the world deems success. Barabbas was so enmeshed in his seeming triumph that he did not look at Jesus. Perchance it was because he was not raised upon a cross that he gained no sight of the Saviour. We are constantly being compelled to choose between what the world pronounces success and what is true success in the eyes of God, though it be failure from the viewpoint of men. Barabbas lacks what Jesus has possessed eternally, a lasting influence for all that is ennobling and righteous and good.

The choice between Barabbas and Jesus confronts every soul as well as every culture and society.

In the familiar poem written during the Mexican War by James Russell Lowell, these moving lines appear:

> Once to every man and nation
> Comes the moment to decide,
> In the strife of truth with falsehood,
> For the good or evil side.
> And the choice goes by forever
> 'Twixt that darkness and that light.

We are faced with choosing between vulgarity, crassness, ignorance and refinement, culture, and the enlightenment afforded by the Christian spirit.

We are confronted with the choice between the easy, devious road of falsehood and compromise with evil — and the hard path of cleaving to the right, no matter what the cost.

We are compelled to decide between the world's way of selfishness, hatred, and vengeance — and Christ's way of love, gentleness magnanimity, and disciplined living.

We must decide between an outlook without hope and without God — and a life of faith in Christ, the God-man, the Saviour of the world, the Lord of life and light.

Barabbas had longed and looked for the kingdom of his people, Israel. When the King was in the midst and he was so very near to Him, even in sight of Him, he missed Him. You can be very close to Christ, hear His words and the voice of His Spirit, and yet continue living as though you had never heard His words or His name.

8

The Cross as an Interruption

> *"And as they came out, they found a man of Cyrene, Simon by name: him they compelled to bear His cross."* MATTHEW 27:32

It was an interruption that overtook Simon of Cyrene. In 1858, Oliver Wendell Holmes, poet and physician, commenced his book of essays, *The Autocrat of the Breakfast Table,* with the clause: "I was just going to say, when I was interrupted." Then Holmes proceeded to relate how a quarter of a century earlier he was interrupted in the preparation of a series of essays. The interruption was of twenty-five years duration for the Harvard medical professor.

I. Interruptions Are Opportunities

Moses was tending his flocks amid the solitariness of the Midianite desert when he was interrupted by the spectacle of a bush that burned yet was not consumed. There on that holy ground, where he was instructed to give due reverence, Moses was called to lead Israel out of the house of bondage and up from slavery to the land God had promised to the forefathers.

A stalwart youth from his father's farm, Saul, son of Kish, standing head and shoulders above his fellows, was on an errand in quest of stray donkeys when he was stopped suddenly in that pedestrian task by the prophet Samuel, who had come to anoint him as Israel's first king.

A shepherd lad from the hills beyond Bethlehem was on an errand for his father, Jesse, bearing provisions and messages for his older brothers in King Saul's army, when he was catapulted from obscurity into the national limelight as he became the vanquisher of the menacing Philistine giant, Goliath. David's emergence into the arena of national fame came as a surprise in the midst of a boy's errand.

When Jesus was hastening to the bedside of a desperately sick child, He was stopped by a nameless woman, a chronic sufferer, who sought to touch the hem of His garment and find healing.

The most flaming foe of the early Christians was rid-ing down the Damascene road, breathing out threaten-ings and slaughter against the messengers of Christ's peace, when there flashed before him "the light of the world" and sounded in his ears, a voice: "I am Jesus whom thou persecutest." Thus it was that Saul of Tarsus was arrested in his ferocious course that he might become Christ's great apostle.

One can fancy a scholarly physician, with a pro-pensity for literature and history as well as science, seated at his desk in his office. Without warning there comes a surprise visit from a scintillating, intriguing little Jew in search of relief from his "oft infirmity." Perchance out of such an interview, Luke, versed in the culture and science of Greece, was won to Christ and entered upon a friendship with St. Paul, which was to receive its crowning tribute in those final, dark days of Rome, when the apostle wrote for the ages: "Only Luke is with me."

Peter was brooding over a vision which impressed upon him the universality and catholicity of the Chris-tian faith, when a knocking at a lower threshold de-noted the appearance of three men, who had come to escort the big fisherman to a Roman centurion, Cor-nelius. Peter was, though he knew it not at the moment of the knocking, destined to lead that noble Roman to repentance towards God and faith in the Lord Jesus Christ.

Said George Mueller: "The stops as well as the steps of a good man are ordered by the Lord."

On several occasions I preached from a pulpit in a city in New York State behind which was a fine memorial window depicting the parable of The Good Samaritan. At the base of the window was an inscription: "The steps of a good man are ordered by the Lord." That certain Samaritan was taken by surprise by the presence of the bandit's victim, bleeding and gasping along the roadside. He interpreted his interruption as an opportunity to respond to a call of human need.

Interruptions bring opportunities for helpfulness as in this supreme instance where the Cyrenian came to the aid of Jesus. When a student apologized to the English scholar and essayist, A. C. Benson, for breaking in upon his time of study, the master of Eton and later at Magdalene College, Cambridge, protested: "I do not relish a compliment to my industry at the expense of my humanity."

Life's interruptions move us to the contemplation of solemn themes, to which we might otherwise accord no heed. Simon was no doubt made sober and pensive by this episode on the Jerusalem street.

> Just when we are safest,
> There's a sunset touch,
> A fancy from a flowerbell, someone's death,
> A chorus ending from Euripides.

In his autobiography, the brilliant but meteoric Philadelphia pulpit orator, Dr. Lawrence M. Colfelt, relates impressions of his student years at Washington and Jefferson College. He reflects on the initial president of the combined colleges, the Rev. Dr. Jonathan Edwards. Dr. Edwards was the intimate friend and preached the funeral sermon in the New York Avenue Presbyterian Church of Washington for Dr. Phineas Densmore Gurley, Lincoln's minister, who preached the sermon at the bier of the sixteenth president. Colfelt describes Edwards as "a little giant in speech with his finely sculptured phrases," and tells how Edwards invariably read from the Psalms in the daily chapel. When he came to that enigmatical word Selah, he always made the sober comment in translation, "Pause and ponder it."

Our lives are interrupted by incidents such as that which befell Simon that we may pause and ponder the deeper truths of life. It may be that such an interruption will bring us, as it did Simon, face to face with Christ. There He stands, saying, "Behold, I stand at the door and knock!"

II. *No Neutrality Before the Cross*

Simon had come to the sidelines as a spectator but he was not allowed to continue in that capacity. He came from a section of North Africa that emerged into prominence during World War II. It is likely that he was of Hebrew lineage and faith, hence, came to the Holy City as a Passover pilgrim. Like the Psalmist, he was saying with inward exultation, "My feet shall stand within thy gates, O Jerusalem. Jerusalem is builded as a city that is compact together: whither the tribes go up, the tribes of the Lord, unto the testimony of Israel, to give thanks unto the name of the Lord." While he came with devout and pious intentions to Jerusalem, Simon may have paused in the throngs with a certain indifference. Momentarily he stood there gazing at the spectacle of Jesus in His suffering under the weight of the cross. Pythagoras, the Greek philosopher and mathematician, wrote of those who attended the Olympic games and were content not to participate but to be spectators of the wonder, the hurry and the magnificence of the scene. No one can remain permanently a detached spectator viewing human need and tribulation. No one can assume the aloof position where misery is concerned. Neither can one remain a dilettantish spectator of Christ and His cross. We look on Lazarus, full of wounds and bruises and putrefying sores, begging at our doorstep. We can simply look at him unmoved with Dives and then go to hell as Dives did one night, there to abide forever with the selfish and self-centered, who refuse to stain their purple and fine linen while ministering to human need. On the other hand, we can follow the Master as He makes haste to descend from the mountainside to heal hearts athrob with pain. There is no neutrality in the face of human suffering. Neither can one remain neutral at the cross.

III.   The Timing of Providence

Simon arrived at the precise spot where Jesus fell under the burden of His cross and the soldiers perceived His inability to carry the cross. Simon might well have come there a moment before. In the parable of The Good Samaritan, Jesus uses the phrase: "And by chance there came down a certain priest that way."

The chances are in the custody of Providence. In the idyllic book of Ruth, the author states of King David's Moabitess ancestress, "and her hap was to light on a part of the field belonging unto Boaz, who was of the kindred of Elimelech." Happenstance is under the control of Him, who knows the end from the beginning. In his provocative novel, *The Bridge of San Luis Rey,* Thornton Wilder wrote of the finest bridge in all Peru, which collapsed on Friday noon, July 20, 1714, and precipitated five travellers, like so many gesticulating ants' into the gulf below. Brother Juniper, a passing priest, arrived near the scene in time to glance at the bridge before it fell and hear the twanging noise as it divided. "Why did this happen to these five?" he questions. "If there were any plan in the universe at all, if there were any pattern to human life, surely it would be discovered mysteriously latent in those lives so suddenly cut off. Either we live by accident and die by accident, or we live by plan and die by plan" (*The Bridge of San Luis Rey,* Thornton Wilder, Grosset and Dunlap, p. 19). Why did these five persons reach the bridge at the very juncture when so melancholy a fate would overtake them?

The most eminent of the Greek apologists for Christianity in the second century was Flavius Justinus, better known as Justin Martyr. Dr. George Tybout Purvis, one of the most recondite and ringing preachers of the Presbyterian church, gave the theological world a strong book on Justin's monumental contribution to the streams of Christian thought. Justin had lived in Samaria but was of Roman or Greek descent and had been educated in Hellenic lore. As a young man he tasted philosophies and as Dr. Philip Schaff tells us, he was "knocking at every gate of ancient wisdom, except the Epicurean, which he despised." One day as he was strolling near the seashore, he encountered and entered into conversation with a stranger, a venerable old Christian of pleasant countenance and gentle dignity. There ensued a conversation which changed the course of Justin's career. The aged man shook Justin's confidence in human philosophy and directed him to an examination of the Hebrew prophets and the light shed on the Old Testament by the Gospels, especially the fulfillment of the Old Testament prophecies in the person and work of Christ. Was it mere chance, uncontrolled by a wiser Hand, unseen of men yet not unknown, which brought into touch with each other a cultured and erudite young scholar and a saintly and learned Christian?

Why did Simon of Cyrene come to a particular locale at an exact point of time and why did the Roman soldiers single him out from the crowd to be requisitioned into service for Christ? Why did you take a seat beside a certain person on a train or bus? Why did you go to a certain church, previously unknown to you, when a minister, equally unknown to you, delivered a sermon peculiarly fitted to answer your questions and solve your problems? "There is a Destiny that shapes our ends."

IV. *The Privilege of Helping Jesus*

At the outset, Simon's deed was one of involuntary kindness. He was pressed into the act by the Roman soldiers. Our age is not a stranger to the involuntary kindness, which is performed for professional, political, and business reasons, and with a view to public opinion. As the involuntary kindness of Simon passed beyond that phase into a sincere work of helpfulness for Jesus, kind acts that originate under pressure and with a measure of superficial urbanity can develop into a spirit of loving, unselfish service.

Simon was granted the privilege of being of great service to Jesus Christ.

In one of her less-known hymns, Mrs. Cecil Frances Alexander says:

> His are the thousand sparkling rills
> That from a thousand fountains burst,
> And fill with music all the hills;
> And yet He saith, "I Thirst."

During His earthly life Jesus permitted many persons to help Him. A nameless soldier ran with a sponge filled with vinegar to relieve his thirst. Martha was allowed to prepare delicious suppers for Him, though He was "the bread of life." He let an unknown farmer offer His beast for Him to ride in the parade, though He was king of all creation. He permitted the family in Bethany to provide Him a home, though He is the "home" of the soul. He allowed Joseph to provide a tomb, although He was the conqueror of the grave. Christ continues to afford us the privilege of serving Him, albeit helping Him in His "body," the church, and in the person of those who have need.

V. Our Inscrutable Cross

It was a cross, which he could not understand and was hard to bear, that was thrust with suddenness upon Simon. Sickness lays a clammy hand upon us and those whom we love in the twinkling of an eye and with no apparent warning. A flash of light, a break of the wave and we are incapacitated. One day the celebrated Dr. John Ker, the Scottish preacher and authority on the history of preaching, awakened to discover himself shorn of the powers of memory. After a considerable lapse of time he regained that faculty, apart from which life is scarcely worth enduring. Recently there appeared a book entitled *The Man Who Lived Twice*. It is the story of a literary and dramatic critic, Edward Sheldon, who in the very noontide of his activities, was reduced swiftly to the status of an invalid. The once-active life was ended. Henceforth for the second portion of his days, confinement to a bed in his room was to be this alert man's lot. That cribbed, cabined and confined province was to become a shrine to which a great host of admirers made their pilgrimages and always with more inspiration and cheer imparted to them than they could bestow on Mr. Sheldon. Our crosses, grievous to be borne, come quickly.

The cross taken from the bleeding back of Jesus and laid on Simon's strong shoulders had an infinitely deeper significance than he could have realized. Is it any less true with our minor crosses?

There is the cross of physical affliction, in which we are called to exemplify the grace and power of Christ, remembering that whom the Lord loveth He chasten-

eth and that our light affliction, which is but for a
moment, worketh for us a far more eternal and ex-
ceeding weight of glory. There is the cross of suffering
reproach for the sake of Christ, holding fast to the
supernatural gospel in an age when naturalism is
popular, living a life of Christian purity, integrity, and
love, while the world offers its supposed prizes to those
who tamper with conscience, regard moral standards
as antiquated, and consider retaliation more manly
than love. There is the cross of standing for principles
in professional, business, and social life, no matter
what cost or derision may be involved. There is the
cross of accepting a hard, unpromising, disheartening
post with meekness and contentment, remaining as did
Titus, by Paul's appointment, amid the unlovely, often
morally disgusting inhabitants of Crete. There is the
cross of renouncing personal plans and ambitions and
entering into the dear Christ's life of sacrifice.

No one ever fully comprehends his cross. Yet we
must recognize, as did Simon of Cyrene, that what may
seem a cruel deprivation and an annoyance of the
worst order, an indignity all undeserved, a trial of
temper and patience, may be a blessing in disguise.
Simon found the cross that he bore the gateway of
life, the means of finding and serving the Saviour.

VI. *Simon's Reward*

Simon received his reward for bearing the cross.
None who serve Jesus go unrewarded. The cup of
cold water extended to a disciple does not pass un-
forgotten. "God is not unrighteous to forget your work

and labor of love." The Samaritan woman, who offered Jesus a drink of water on a frightfully hot noon, received the infinitely greater gift of the "water of life" to satisfy forever the soul's immortal longings. A home in Capernaum, which offered Jesus a Sabbath day's hospitality, was made to be filled with rejoicing for the healing brought to a loved one. A woman, who lavished upon Him the tribute of rare perfume, received the benediction of His everlasting memorial of her act of loving devotion. It would have been sufficient recompense for Simon to have had the glorious satisfaction of having been of some service to Christ. St. Mark identifies Simon as the father of Alexander and Rufus. When a man finds Christ, untold influences are released into the hearts of those near to him. Simon had the joy of having his sons in the service of Christ. Others have had, if not in this world, then yonder on the battlements of heaven, the joy of witnessing, if not their immediate children, their grandchildren and more remote descendants, numbered among the ministers and active servants of the Christ.

The Christ of the cross may come suddenly into your life. Will you respond to Him, saying, "Dear Saviour, enter, enter and leave us nevermore!"

9

Emotion on the Road to the Cross

> *"But Jesus turning unto them said, Daughters of Jerusalem, weep not for me, but weep for yourselves, and for your children."*
>
> LUKE 23:28

Tears were shed in the presence of Jesus on a succession of occasions.

A woman, befouled by sin but moved now with contrition, wept as she anointed the Saviour's feet with precious ointment and bathed them with the flowing tresses of her hair.

Professional mourners emitted wild, Oriental wails over the fair young daughter of Jairus as she reposed in the sleep of death in her own bedroom. Their lugubrious cries filled the house until Jesus promptly dismissed them, saying, "She is not dead, but sleepeth."

Peter, as the fountain of the great deep in his nature was broken up by the glance of Jesus following his denial, wept bitterly.

Mary of Magdala, arriving in the garden of the Arimathaean before the dawn's early light, supposed Jesus to be the gardener and was visibly affected as the risen Master inquired of her, "Woman, why weepest thou?"

Washington Irving said: "There is a sacredness in tears. They are not the mark of weakness, but of power. They speak more eloquently than ten thousand tongues. They are the messengers of overwhelming grief, of deep contrition, and of unspeakable love."

Jesus Himself was known to weep. Standing in a suburban cemetery at Bethany with those two disconsolate sisters, Mary and Martha, He wept audibly at the tomb of Lazarus. He was appalled at the stark tragedy of death.

On the purple brow of Olivet with the Holy City gleaming before His gaze, Jesus mingled His lamentations with the cheers of the populace, who acclaimed Him with their glad hosannas.

The author of the Epistle to the Hebrews comments that "strong crying and tears" marked the midnight vigil in Gethsemane on the eve of the cross.

The tear most sacred, shed for others' pain
That starts at once, bright, pure from pity's mine,
Already polished by the Hand Divine.

This was the tear which coursed down the cheeks of the women of Jerusalem. The Via Dolorosa had its surging emotion in the tears of a large company of the working women of Jerusalem. They knew the drudgery of daily toil. They were animated by pity for Jesus. They had heard His words of infinite compassion. Some of them and their children had been recipients of His miracles of mercy. He had imposed hands of blessing upon the heads of their children, whom they brought to Him. They "bewailed and lamented" and "wondered in sad surprise" as the Man of Sorrows, acquainted with grief was led forth to execution. They were shocked at the thought of the innocent and incomparably kind Jesus being subjected to such injustice and barbarity. They had a tragic sense concerning one so young being cut off out of the land of the living, when "not one golden hair was gray on His crucifixion day." In the original version of the hymn, which Matthew Arnold on the last day of his life called the noblest hymn of the English language, Isaac Watts refers to Jesus as "the young Prince of Glory."

While they weep for Jesus falling under the weight of His cross He regards them with equal if not deeper tenderness and pity.

He finds in this company of women an earnest of the devotion that women through all succeeding ages would give Him.

There is no record of any woman failing or opposing Jesus. The Hungarian artist, Munkacsy, in his *Christ before Pilate,* relieves the harshness of the trial scene by the figure of a young mother, a working woman of Jerusalem, holding in her arms a man child, who may have been a recipient of His healing grace and virtue. With His relentless foes ranged against Him, she reflects only sympathy. It was from a woman that Jesus first learned the revealed religion of Israel. It was a woman who devoutly acknowledged Him as the Messiah when He came suddenly to the temple as an infant. It was the generous women of Palestine who supported His ministry and "ministered to Him of their substance." It was a woman who anointed Him for burial. There were two women who provided the retreat to which He repaired repeatedly for refreshment, especially on those final evenings. Women assisted in preparing His broken body for burial with spices and fine linen. Women were earliest in coming to pay love's tribute at His sepulchre. It was to them that He made His initial appearance in the splendor of His resurrection body. On but one occasion did Jesus rebuke a woman, and that an effusive person, who in maudlin, unrestrained fashion sought to heap adulation upon Him and His mother. Through the centuries, women have been the loyal, devoted friends of Jesus.

One of the exceptional characters of mid nineteenth

century New England was the learned blacksmith, Elihu Burrit of New Britain, Connecticut. Though afforded only a common schooling, with native genius, an insatiable thirst for knowledge, and the voracious reading, which is the best method of self-education, he became one of the most prodigiously erudite persons of his age, as well as an accomplished linguist, humanitarian, philanthropist, and pioneer champion of international peace. Longfellow observed that nothing ever came from his pen that was not wholesome and good. Elihu Burrit paid a touching tribute to his mother at her grave, saying, as he thought of her as a friend of the Lord Jesus: "Our godly, beloved mother, who to all her children, both on earth and in heaven, was the most precious friend this side of Jesus Christ. My godly mother, whose prayers seem at times to surround me like a worshipping atmosphere."

In a letter to the wife of the Amherst professor of astronomy, who was to be, with her daughter, one of her biographers, Emily Dickinson wrote in 1885, the year before her passing, to the younger friend then on a European tour, this unique tribute to the Christ: "The Saviour's only signature to the letter He wrote to all mankind was, 'a stranger and ye took me in.' "

Women have been among Christ's most enthusiastic friends and have led many other friends to His side.

Jesus felt a kinship with those women who toiled daily for their livelihood. Theirs was a fellowship of self-denial, self-renunciation, and self-sacrifice. The historian Lecky said that the history of self-sacrifice is the history of Christianity. These women had been compelled to bear their crosses through the world. Jesus envisages more frightful agonies yet to descend upon them. With prophetic insight, He describes that abomination of desolation, which would come in the year seventy under the armies of the Roman emperor Titus. He knows that it has been the women of the world who have felt most acutely the sufferings of war. Long ago, the Greek dramatist, Sophocles, illustrated this fact in the tragic figure of Antigone. In *Vanity Fair*, Thackeray describes the solicitous women in the city of Brussels while the Battle of Waterloo was transpiring. He writes of a dull distant din heard in the city and coming from the south and then a thousand pale and anxious faces looking from casements of the city's homes. Then ensued the anxiety of the women through the days of raging battle. All day long on the Sabbath, while the women were praying, ten miles away the battle continued. In one of the most dramatic sentences in English literature, Thackeray concludes the chapter: "No more firing was heard at Brussels — the pursuit rolled miles away. Darkness came down on the field and city and Amelia was praying for George, who was lying on his face, dead, with a bullet through his heart."

During our own Civil War, Thomas Buchanan Reade wrote on *The Brave at Home* in one of his poems and spoke of the woman left behind:

Doomed nightly in her dreams to hear
The bolts of death around him rattle.

At the timeof the First World War, John Oxenham

wrote in England *A Little Te Deum for Womanhood,*
enduring the strains of that era:

We thank Thee, Lord, for Thy sweet Heart
    of Grace
Revealed in womanhood in these black days:
For her high courage under bitter stress;
For her new spheres of wondrous usefulness;
For her heroic fortitude in loss;
For her most patient bearing of her cross;
For her high seizure of the times' dire needs;
For her sweet sum of self-denying deeds;
For her self-adaptation to the claims
Of these new days; . . . .
For the grace of heart and life and winning face
To young lives broken in the fiery race;
. . . .
Heart thanks and praise we render, Lord, to Thee.

In their deep emotion these women of Jerusalem
wrested from Jesus an apocalypse of His own attitudes.
Their presence and His response show Him as He
submerged His own sorrow and suffering by concern
for the pain of others. Jesus surmounted the worst
that anguish can do to the personality as He thought,
not of Himself in fruitless self-pity, but of others.
The humdrum of life for these poor women lining
the route of His march to Calvary was to culminate
in the horrors of the siege of the year 70. Josephus, the
physician-historian, was to reflect on the heroism of
these women and others, when he observed: "There
has never been a race on earth, and there never will
be one, whose sufferings can be matched with those

of Jerusalem in the days of the siege." In addition to these women, Jesus diverted His thought from His own pain as the cross was reached, by looking away from Himself to His enemies, who with grim gratification watched the ghastly processes of crucifixion as the goal of their diabolical designs; to the Roman soldiers, who, as they obeyed orders, knew not what they did; and to His aging mother and her desolate future, which John might make easier and brighter; and a wreck of a man, begging for mercy in the life that follows life. Jesus triumphed over His own troubles as He sought to be pitiful and compassionate towards the tragedy in other lives.

Jesus was a fervent patriot. He divulged His passionate love of the City of the Great King and His own, His native land as He described the shape of things to come. With the redemption of the world and personal tragedy combining to engage His thought, He was stirred by the sight of the capital city of His nation. To those who protest when we introduce the note of patriotism, our country, her present state, and future role, we would cite the example of Jesus. "O Jerusalem! Jerusalem!" We hear Him expressing patriotic sentiments under the shadow of the atoning cross, which came as the very crown and climax of His ministry and incarnate life.

By his attitude towards these lachrymose women, Jesus discloses His view concerning emotion with respect to Himself. "Daughters of Jerusalem, weep not for me but for yourselves and for your children!" He appends a fragment of a parable, "For if they do these things in a green tree, what shall be done in the dry?" If the wicked rulers of Jerusalem and Rome visit so terrible a fate upon Jesus in the innocence and strength of His young manhood, what will the cruel rulers of Rome do as the agents of divine judgment and retribution on the people that refused their day of opportunity to accept God's love in Christ and have thereby fallen into a state of spiritual destitution?

In the day of ultimate reckoning, our emotions and sentiments entertained concerning Jesus, however pious they may have been, will not suffice. Jesus does not desire us to luxuriate in religious sentiment concerning Him and His cross. He longs to see tears, not of pity for Him in the spectacle of His suffering, but of contrition for our sins and of surrender to His claims on our souls. He is eager to see within us searchings of conscience and the exercise of faith in Him as the Redeemer from sin that will fructify in a character conformed to His will.

Ah, well that we should be shaken emotionally as we stand afar and gaze upon Jesus, crowned with thorns and nailed to His cross. Far better is it and more pleasing to Him when the contemplation of that scene should induce within us the sorrow that leads to repentance and the faith in His blood that saves from sin and issues in the changed life, inspired by Him who died that we should no longer live unto ourselves but unto Him, who died for us.

10

The Gamblers at Golgotha

"And they crucified him (Jesus), and parted his garments, casting lots: that it might be fulfilled which was spoken by the prophet, They parted my garments among them, and upon my vesture did they cast lots." MATTHEW 27:35

The Roman soldiers, who supervised the crucifixion of Jesus, exercised the prerogative of the executioners of that age concerning the clothing and personal property of a condemned man. They divested Jesus of His garments and then resorted to the ancient practice of lewd fellows of the baser sort, namely, gambling. They cast lots over the Saviour's meager possessions. They marvelled at the seamless robe, which may have been fashioned by His mother or some of the devoted women who ministered to Him. In his Gospel, St. Matthew relates that this act of stripping Jesus of His robes and then casting lots for them, though in itself so fraught with cheapness and meanness, was in direct fulfillment of a prophecy recorded centuries earlier in Psalm 22, with supernatural insight, and, predicting the very incidents of the day of the cross. The Psalmist said: "They parted my garments among them and cast lots upon my vesture." "Known unto God are all His works from the beginning of the world." This divine foreknowledge and foreordination was especially true with respect to the events attendant upon the cross and atoning sacrifice of the Son of God. It was concerning this scene of the gambling at Golgotha that the writer of the Epistle to the Hebrews was reflecting when he mentioned those who "crucify the Son of God afresh and put Him to an open shame."

Men still divide Christ's garments among them. They seize the gifts and influences of Jesus and the by-products of Christianity. Then, like the gambling soldiers on Calvary's brow, they leave Christ on His cross, ignored, rejected, naked, humiliated, regarded as "a dead fact stranded on the shore of the oblivious years." The Book of Common Prayer of the Anglican communion speaks of "all other benefits of Christ's passion" in addition to our redemption from sin and death. The modern counterparts of the soldiers of Rome appropriate as their very own these other benefits, meanwhile repudiating the deity of Jesus, turning their backs on His divine presence, and spurning His claims. They remain oblivious to the mystery of His atonement for our sins. They feel no sense of obligation to Christ's church, which He founded, purchased with His precious blood, and through whose medium He transmits the blessings of His spiritual reign to the world. They decline to enter into any personal relationship with Christ as their Saviour and their God. They fail to appreciate Christ as the virtual fountainhead of the finest gifts of our culture.

What are some of the garments of Christ which a world rejecting Him and His deity and Saviourhood appropriates?

I.

They take the garment of His philanthropy and humanitarianism. A New York journalist, Charles Loring Brace, in his remarkable volume *Gesta Christi* traces the histor yof humane institutions to their inception under the impetus of the Spirit of Christ. There were no hospitals until Christians established the earliest institutions for the sick in Rome and Constantinople. There were no asylums for the mentally afflicted until Christ's spirit was let loose in the world. When Jesus came into the world those who were deranged, as the Gospels show, were forced to have their habitat among the gloomy tenements of the dead. Clara Barton and her associates chose the cross as the emblem for the army of mercy, always first on the scene of disaster. It was inevitable that when the gospel of Christ was being proclaimed in the south by the Wesleys and Whitefield, orphanages for the children, to whom Jesus gave such tender consideration, should be founded.

Men of our modern world continue to divide Christ's garments in the hospitals, charities, eleemosynary institutions begotten of His Spirit. Meanwhile they fail to acknowledge that none of these agencies could exist had it not been for Him who went through the cities and villages of Palestine healing all manner of diseases, telling His Parable of the Good Samaritan, and identifying Himself, the merciful Saviour with the most forgotten man among the world's sufferers.

II.

Modern men, while denying the Christ of God, take the right of every man to a higher education, one of the garments of Jesus.

When Peter emerged from the upper room on the Day of Pentecost and began to preach to the multitudes on the streets of Jerusalem, he enunciated the deep truths of God to ordinary men and women. He spoke in language which assured them that there was in the common man of that throng the power of understanding, judging, and deciding questions, which had hitherto been the sacred custody of ecclesiastics and theologians. As Phillips Brooks, speaking on the influence of Jesus, told a group of divinity students in Philadelphia years ago: "There was nothing like that speech of Peter's before that day. The germs of the modern lecture and the modern school were in it. Thenceforth men's intellects might differ, but the intellectual chance was open to every man. To the dullest child belong the right to learn all that he could learn, all that was in him to learn of God and His world."

The great ancient universities on the continent, Oxford and Cambridge and the Sorbonne, were established under the auspices of the Christian church. Harvard, our oldest institution of learning, was begun when a minister of the gospel bequeathed his library for a school and there was realized the need of an educated clergy. Yale had its inception under the trusteeship of the ten principal ministers of the colony of Connecticut. Princeton traces roots to a log cabin college on the banks of the Neshaminy in Bucks County, Pennsylvania, where it was presided over by a Presbyterian minister, and later by a long and eminent succession of Presbyterian divines, who led the college at Elizabeth and Princeton. In Philadelphia the oldest university has on its campus the statue of a flaming evangelist, who with other ministers of Christ laid the foundation. The majority of our institutions of higher learning had their inception through the church.

The modern public school traces its history to John Calvin and the schools which he instituted in the city of Geneva, Switzerland, with its theocratic government under his sway.

The freedom of scientific research issues from the right of the individual to have unrestricted access to all knowledge in whatever form it may be found. That liberty had its fount in Christianity and its flowering in the spirit of the Protestant Reformation.

We sometimes overlook the great boon to social progress and human happiness which emanates from freedom from superstition. Christian missionaries in earlier years went to the Indians of our nation, teaching them Christ's gospel and affording an education which emancipated them from their benighted condition and bondage to the fears of paganism. Albert Schweitzer cites as one of Christianity's principal contributions to the dark continent, the liberation that it has brought to those who were enslaved by superstition and the incantations of witch doctors. Men overcome their superstitions and advance in an intelligent, reasonable approach to life when they have as their leader, Jesus, who in enforcing one of His great lessons, said, "Consider the ravens." With much daring he used as a figure the raven, long regarded as a bird of ill omen. He repudiated by that figure the groundless superstitions which exist where the light of His truth has not penetrated. Superstitions can have no place in a world conceived from a Christian viewpoint as governed and pervaded by the power and presence of the God of love and infinite intelligence.

Men take Christ's gifts and influences in the rights and opportunities of education. Then they disregard Him, who said, "I am the truth." "Ye shall know the truth, and the truth shall make you free."

III.

Modern men treasure the literature, which is a part of the heritage of Christian faith, while they refuse to accept the Christ, who is the inspiration thereof.

If you were to exscind the influence and name of Christ from literature, you would have to remove the force exerted by the majestic King James version of the Bible in moulding our speech in its golden forms. You would no longer have the first great autobiography of the modern world, a document of the highest import for the student of psychology, the Confessions of St. Augustine, who was described by Adolph Harnack of Berlin as the first modern man. You would have to eliminate Tasso and Dante and Pascal and á Kempis.

In our English literature it would be necessary to destroy such early fragments as Cynewulf and Caedmon and the Venerable Bede, Alfred the Great, the legends of the Holy Grail, Langland's Piers Ploughman and considerable sections of Chaucer, who alluded to Christ as "the first stock father of gentleness." You would have to consign Bunyan to oblivion, delete long passages from Spenser and Shakespeare and Milton. De Foe's *Robinson Crusoe* would take its exit from our English classics. John Donne would be gone. Much would be missing from the novels of George Eliot and Walter Scott and Dickens and Hawthorne. The poetry of Tennyson, Browning, Lowell, to mention only a few, would be reduced immeasurably.

Speaking not long since in one of our universities,

a student challenged me to name any traces of Biblical or Christian teaching in the modern novelists, John Steinbeck in particular. I recalled that two of Steinbeck's best-known works bore Biblical titles, *East of Eden,* and *Grapes of Wrath.* One of the most cynical books of recent years bore the unmistakable New Testament title, *Generation of Vipers.*

In Dickens' *Dombey and Son,* we are told how Harriet Dombey read "the Eternal Book for all the weary and heavy laden, for all the wretched, fallen, and neglected of this earth — read the blessed history, in which the blind, lame, palsied beggar, the criminal, the woman stained with shame, the shunned of all our dainty clay, has each a portion, that no human pride, indifference, or sophistry through all the ages that this world shall last, can take away, or by the thousandth atom of a grain reduce — read the ministry of Him, who through the round of human life, and all its hopes and griefs, from birth to death, from infancy to age, had sweet compassion for, and interest in, its every scene and stage, its every suffering and sorrow."

Like Dickens, the world's greatest authors, and especially those of our English speaking world, have recognized their profound indebtedness to the Bible and their high inspiration from Christ and the Christian religion.

IV.

The world outside the faith of Christ and His church takes the fine arts, one of Christ's garments, and divides the treasures of that realm, remaining thoughtless of Christ and His spiritual kingdom.

In the miracle play produced by the church to dramatize Biblical episodes and convey religious truths, there was the genesis of much of modern drama as well as the oratorio and the opera. It was a priest and social worker in Rome, Philip Neri, who, in order to solve the problem created by youthful leisure and unemployment, originated in the oratory (the place of prayer) of his religious order, the oratorio, out of which the opera came as a later development.

If you were to omit Christian influences in music, it would be necessary to dispose of Bach and much of Brahms and Palestrina, Handel and Mozart and Verdi and Gounod.

Father Walsh, a Roman Catholic priest, in an informing volume, *The World's Debt to the Catholic Church,* declares that the cult of the beautiful has its chief debt to the church in the province of architecture. What would architecture be without the Gothic, largely cultivated in Christian church circles; the meeting houses of New England with their spires pointing heavenward; and the mighty cathedrals, the masterpieces of architecture in all the ages?

In painting, the greatest canvases have to do with Christian themes. Witness the work of Raphael, Botticelli, Leonardo da Vinci, Rembrandt, and the Pre-Raphaelites, to mention only a few.

In sculpture, a Michelangelo and a Thorwaldsen

chose the great subjects of the Bible and the Christian faith.

Art is replete with reminders of what Christ and Christianity have meant to the world and, in particular, to those who prize and cultivate the beautiful.

V.

Our political heritage is one of Christ's garments appropriated by a world that makes meager acknowledgment of His kingship over the nations and His church, to which all who honor public morality and decency owe an obligation.

All that remains of Jamestown, Virginia, is the church tower, emblem of the church and her honored position in that early American society. The love of liberty created by the spirit of Christ in the human heart was brought here by the Pilgrims, the Puritans, the Scotch and Scotch-Irish of Pennsylvania and the Carolinas, the Quakers, and the other contributing groups at the dawn of our national life.

Einstein, who had no affiliation with the Christian church, observed with appreciation that it was not the exponents of freedom in the academic circles of Germany who were the most persevering defenders of human freedom against the crushing force of Nazism, but the leaders of the Christian church.

Christianity filled the world with a new evaluation of the infinite dignity and sacredness of the humblest individual and that political freedom which is his inalienable right. Multitudes, alas, thrive in such a social and political climate and contribute nothing to support the cause and church, out of which this concept issues, like streams of the temple, which Ezekiel in his vision noted, as they flowed out from the sanctuary, expanded, deepened, widened, and brought life, prosperity and blessing to the world.

There is the moral influence of Christianity felt far beyond the pale of those who ascribe salvation to Christ as the Lamb slain for our sins.

There are those who question the cardinal truths of Christianity, selecting what they will of the Sermon on the Mount, the Golden Rule, the Christian social ideals of chivalry and courtesy, the elevation of womanhood and childhood, the abolition of human slavery. There are many who respond to the stimulus Christ imparts to those who would do good to their fellow men, devoting themselves to the most sacrificial service. They discover an interest in people whom the world generally would deem unattractive and uninteresting. Who save a Christian poet would have written:

> He who feels contempt
> For any living thing, hath faculties
> That he hath never used: and
> Thought with him
> Is in its infancy.

There are those who take Jesus' humane idealism; yet one hears Mary's plaintive cry, "They have taken away my Lord, and I know not where they have laid Him." They want Jesus' morals and mercy but not His mystery. They disdain climbing that hill of expiatory sacrifice called Calvary.

Many live, as Carlyle confessed of himelf, in the "after shine" of their parents' and ancestors' Christian faith.

In his autobiography, the late Dr. George Frederick Wright, a Congregational minister and long a professor in Oberlin College, where among other subjects he taught geology, tells how at the age of twelve he united with the Congregational church in a New York State village. Although he was to become a minister notable for being sound in his doctrine, he admits that in that boyhood period he gave his assent to a creedal statement of some length, as pronounced by the pastors, with very scant comprehension of the faith to which he was subscribing. "All that I knew," said Dr. Wright, "was that it was the faith of the best people with whom I was acquainted and I judged the tree by its fruits."

Many know Christianity, as mediated and interpreted to them by loved ones and teachers and early friends, as the noblest influence which has entered into the shaping of their characters. Yet they withhold a confession of faith in their loved ones' Saviour and a tie with the church, which transmits His benefits to the world.

Speaking in St. Paul's Cathedral in London eighty years ago, Dean R. W. Church commented that while darkened days have fallen upon Christendom and society seemed to be disintegrating as it did finally in pagan Rome, the tide has always begun to turn and the terrible disease of public and stagnant despair, which killed Roman society, has never had the mastery in Christendom.

Men are willing to take the note of hopefulness which the Christian faith bestows in the most shadowed hours of history, leaving Christ, the hope of the world, alone on the cross in the darkness.

There is no one in America or in any portion of the world where the gospel in its purity has been proclaimed who has not enjoyed some of the benefits proceeding from Christ, the Lord and life of humanity, who said: "I am come that they might have life and that they might have it more abundantly."

Will you continue to take the benefits proffered by Christ while ignoring Him in His deity and atoning sacrifice as did the coarsened soldiers of pagan Rome? Will you not bow in awe and wonder and loving devotion before the Christ of the cross, the Christ of God, who died to save us from our sins and came to regenerate society as well as sinners, leaving the world forever better and nobler because He passed our mortal way? Will you not bow in penitence and faith at the foot of His cross and rise to discharge your personal obligation to Him in His church?

We hear Him as He says to a world enjoying the blessings that abound whereever He is known: "Have I been so long time with you, and yet hast thou not known me?"

"I died for you, my children, and will ye treat me so?"

11

The Impenitent One

"And there were also two other,
malefactors, led with him to be put to death."

There were three crosses on Calvary. Of the central
cross, Christian believers join with the Apostle Paul
in exclaiming, "God forbid that I should glory, save
in the cross of our Lord Jesus Christ." Of the cross on
which there was nailed the thief, who became penitent,

Christians everywhere sing in Cowper's lines:

> The dying thief rejoiced to see
> That fountain in his day;
> And there may I, though vile as he,
> Wash all my sins away.

Of the other cross and the man who was crucified thereon silence largely prevails.

> Three men shared death upon a hill,
> But only one man died;
> The other two
> A thief and God Himself
> Made rendezvous.
> Three crosses still
> Are borne up Calvary's hill,
> Where sin still lifts them high;
> Upon the one, sag broken men
> Who, cursing, die;
> Another holds the praying thief.
> Or those, who, penitent as he,
> Still find the Christ
> Beside them on the tree.
>   — MIRIAM LeFEVRE CROUSE

The cross of the impenitent malefactor is not without its distinctive though solemn and awful symbolism.

I.

The fact that one of the malefactors, a hardened criminal and bandit, went to his execution affords the assurance that sin is often punished drastically in this life. We hear much about the prosperity of the wicked, a problem that vexed the Hebrew Psalmist and has never ceased to puzzle the thoughtful. We observe the evil men grow gray in their iniquity and seem to flourish like the green bay tree, with no apparent penalty shadowing their nefarious careers. President M. Woolsey Stryker, of Hamilton College, once said: "Sodom does not always burn; not every Korah fats the jaws of the earth" (p. 33, *The Well by the Gate*, M. W. Stryker, *Presbyterian Pulpit Series*). Here is a cross and an executed man demonstrating for all ages that crime does not pay, and that evil more often brings destruction upon the evildoer than it fails so to do. Here is a gallows proclaiming to mankind that the Bible is correct in its stern pronouncements: "The way of the transgressor is hard." "The wicked shall not live out half their days," "Be not deceived; God is not mocked: for whatsoever a man soweth, that shall he also reap." "They have sown the wind, and they shall reap the whirlwind." "He that soweth to the flesh shall of the flesh reap corruption." "Be sure your sins will find you out." "Sin, when it is finished, brings forth death."

Out of the deep during his confinement in Reading Gaol, Oscar Wilde testified:

> The iron gin that waits for sin
> Had caught us in its coil.

"We receive the due reward of our deeds," was the comment of the thief who repented, to his companion on the opposite side of Christ. A man's sins become the Frankenstein monster that accomplishes his undoing. There are more occasions where retribution for wickedness is realized in this world than when it is absent.

II.

The impenitent thief went out into the darkness of eternity with many inducements to repentance towards God, to which he made no slightest response, waiting to arrest his downward course.

In his penetrating study of the unrepentant malefactor, Frederick W. Robertson of Brighton, says: "Round the cross of the dying thief were accumulated such means as never before met together to bring a man to God."

What were some of those circumstances which seemed peculiarly designed to lead a soul to God in contrition and faith?

There was the power of pain "often exerted in the soul to soften it."

> Out of my stony griefs
> Bethel I'll raise;
> So by my woes to be
> Nearer, my God, to Thee.

When he had tasted virtually all of his appointed cup of suffering and with a dread malignancy penetrating the inner recesses of his cranium, one of the accomplished scholars and leaders of the Presbyterian church, who died a score of years ago, told his friends that he would never exchange his last months of agony for any healthier days, so enriching had the last days proved in deepened insights in the things of the Spirit and the nature and will of God.

Alas, to the impenitent thief, suffering was not a savor of life unto life but of death unto death.

He was equally unmoved when he listened to the truth as it was preached by a very recent convert, his comrade in the anguish of crucifixion. Although the "intensity and earnestness of fresh love" characterized the pleas, this man was not stirred.

He had the unequalled privilege of hearing the truth preached from the lips of a dying man. The penitent thief exemplified the phrase of Baxter, the Puritan divine, who said that he always preached as never sure to preach again, a dying man to dying men.

He had the Lord Jesus Himself beside him in the hour of his death. He listened to what Alfred North Whitehead calls in his *Adventures of Ideas,* "the tender words as life ebbed." He hears what John Mason Neale, as he asked the great doctors of the early church in one of his hymns how to gain the lore by which they established the truth, has them reply:

> Dying gift of dying Master,
> Which once uttered all was o'er;
> Pillars seven of sevenfold wisdom.
> Sion's safeguard evermore.

This man, after a lifetime of crime, might have witnessed the majestic serenity and compassion that was Christ's in His dying.

With all of these encouragements to contrition and faith, this man was dead and dumb and blind to God, his own immortal soul's welfare, and his terrible need of redemption from sin. No man ever leaves the world, dying in his sins, to use Christ's own phrase, except as he has had repeated opportunities to forsake his wicked way, abandon his unrighteous thought, and turn to the God who will have mercy and abundantly pardon.

III.

The impenitent thief had no sense of the sacred. "Dost thou not fear God?" was the question put to him by the thief who repented. Reverence was unknown to him.

In his *Science and Philosophy,* Dr. William E. Hocking, of the philosophy department of Harvard, challenges the moral right of the psychoanalyst to probe the deapths of what should be an inviolate province reserved for a man and his God alone. Hocking's position is well taken but one does not have to penetrate very deeply into the inner life of the impenitent robber to realize that this man had no regard for the eternal and invisible realities. He was enmeshed in temporalities. Witness his mad shriek to Jesus: "Save Thyself and us!" He was concerned solely with an extension of life in this world. For a lifetime he had entertained no respect for the personalities and the bodies of his fellow men. He was determined only to exploit them. His irreverence reached the stage of vile derision and raillery. Cursing, blaspheming, sneering, raving, full of acrid mockery, he departs from the world.

Every generation has its ribald purveyors of bitter scorn at the Christian religion, ranging from those in the train of Celsus and Porphyry, who with sarcasm yet literary finesse attack the faith, to others, who in cheap and vulgar form, borrowed from long passé champions of unbelief, pour their contempt on all that is high and holy.

A wave of irreverence has swept over the modern world. You witness it in the theatre, in current fiction, and on the street. You find it in the widespread lawlessness and juvenile delinquency. It is to be noted in a marked degree in the desecration of the Sabbath Day and in the unabashed profanation in public of the hallowed names of the Trinity. You find it in vandalism visited upon cemeteries, works of art, and the shameful lack of regard at times of supposed leaders of our churches for the sanctities of the sanctuary, the appointments of pulpit and chancel, and the beautiful memorials that bespeak the devotion of generations past.

There are persons who have occupied positions of influence in the Christian church, yet who have treated the Bible as though it were a mere document of human literature, rather than the Word of God and a revelation of a supernatural character, which the unaided reason of man could not ascertain.

We find the same lack of reverence in persons who view with contempt those of other races and nations and differing religious views. The modern world and even the church itself stands in need of a revival of reverence.

IV.

This man hanging on his cross, with no word of sorrow for his sin and no importuning of mercy from his Saviour, is a warning concerning the perils of late repentance. The penitent thief has long been regarded as the supreme example of deathbed repentance. Here is the proof that not every man in what Dr. Francis Landey Patton once called the toxic twilight of life's day, turns to his God for absolution and acceptance.

Here was one who had never troubled himself about the spiritual phase of his existence. What did he care for the soul, whether his own or that of his neighbor, whom he viewed as a prospect for one of his acts of brigandage. He may have seen Jesus and heard Him preach. Always he believed, it may have been, that He was an impressive impostor or a poetic dreamer. Surely, he thought within himself, Jesus had nothing to offer him in his situation. The opinions of the years became fixed. Robertson, writing while in his thirties, contended in one of his sermons that opinions are rarely altered after one attains the age of forty. That is, of course, a mooted question. It is certain that a dulling rigidity marks the intellects of men as the years increase. Hostility to new ideas intensifies. Then at length weakness ensues, leaving no strength for vigorous and serious thought on life's deepest issues.

Some persons are never granted what might be termed a dying hour. Without premonition, and in the twinkling of an eye, they lapse into a comatose state or pass suddenly through the gate of death itself.

It was of this melancholy fate of meeting the unseen unfit and unrepentant that the Anglican litany speaks in the petition, "From sudden death, good Lord, deliver us."

Most persons die as they have lived. A Cleveland, Ohio, poet, Edmund Vance Cooke, wrote:

Death comes with a crawl, or comes with a pounce,
And whether he's slow or spry,
It isn't the fact that you're dead that counts,
But only, how did you die?

> — from *Impertinent Poems,*
> DODGE PUBLISHING CO. 1907

It is the manner in which you have lived and thought in active years which will probably govern the fashion in which you will confront death. We must ask ourselves if we are living as we would wish to be when the summons comes for us to confront God and eternity.

The twilight shadows enfold Calvary and a Saviour, who has finished His propitiatory sacrifice, and a man who, following a life of violence, found the homeward way, the Redeemer's love and peace at the last. The shadows also encompass a man whose envenomed and godless tongue was active until the end and who faced death without hope and without God. He had been so impervious to the motions of conscience and the voice of God directed to his soul that for him conscience became insensitive. "Dost not thou fear God?" There is no sensible response from this man.

The Old Testament portrays the disintegrating personality of King Saul who again and again spurned the counsel of the prophet Samuel, who was God's special messenger to his soul. At length, Samuel withdrew from Saul. "Samuel called no more to see Saul until the day of his death." That is parabolic of the relationship between the Holy Spirit and the soul. When one constantly resists the motions of the Divine Spirit, a point of no return is reached.

There is that sometimes baffling passage which tells that God hardened Pharaoh's heart. Pharaoh so persistently declined to give heed to God's voice as mediated by His oracle, Moses, and through the signs and wonders by which God sought to speak to him that at last the Spirit of God withdrew. There was, henceforth, no susceptibility on the Egyptian ruler's part to the suggestions of the Divine.

"Today, if ye would hear his voice, harden not your hearts." "Now is the accepted time; now is the day of salvation."

On which side of the cross of Jesus do you take your stand? Are you on the side of the man who repented, or are you on the side of the man who did not repent?

No one of us need find himself in the plight of this unhappy man. God waits for our confession of sin and faith. Will you go down to the end of your days as this man? Or will you look to the cross of Jesus and say as the penitent thief might well have said:

My sin — oh, the bliss of this glorious thought —

My sin — not in part, but the whole,
Is nailed to the cross and I bear it no more,
Praise the Lord, praise the Lord, O my soul!

                — H. G. Spafford

12

This Was the Son of God

*"And when the centurion,
which stood over against him, saw that he so cried
out, and gave up the ghost, he said, Truly this man
was the Son of God."* MARK 15:39

That was an altogether fitting summary of the life
and death of Jesus. The twilight shadows fell. An awesome hush followed the vibrations of the earth. The

principal, unbiased •witness at the cross uttered his impressions.

Observe this man and the company to which he belonged. The centurion was a Roman army officer and a veteran in the emperor's service. One can imagine that this man may have accompanied the temple police, the soldiers from the Roman fort, and the religious officials as with swords and staves they came to the gate of the garden for the purpose of arresting Jesus. He served in command of the guard having oversight of Jesus in the succession of illicit hearings and trials before Annas and Caiaphas and Pilate and Herod. He may have been the officer who conveyed to Pilate the pleading message of his wife that he was to have nothing to do with this just man, Jesus, because she had suffered many things that night in a dream related to Him. It was he who gave the marching orders to the soldiers as the procession wended its way to the hill outside the city wall. It was by his directive that the soldiers nailed Jesus to the cross.

The New Testament contains a gallery of four Roman centurions. Each was of an admirable character. Canon J. B. Mozley in a justly celebrated sermon at Oxford in the later nineteenth century called his hearers' attention to the absence of all disparagement of the military life in the New Testament.

Although the moral corruption gnawing at the vitals of Roman society was very great and had infiltrated the common soldiery, it had not as yet vitiated the caliber

of the high ranking army officers. The officers continued to exemplify the flower of honor and chivalry in
the most dauntless army of ancient history, having
a proud record of seven centuries of valor. The great
traditions of Rome's past, although declined in other
fields, were maintained by the officers of the army.
Dean Charles Merivale of the cathedral at Ely, England, was, in his extensive history of ancient Rome,
disposed to glorify overmuch the grandeur that was
Rome. He does afford us an imposing picture of the
officers of the Roman army in the era of the crucifixion. Said Dean Merivale: "The history of the Caesars
presents to us a constant succession of brave, patient,
resolute, and faithful soldiers, men deeply impressed
with a sense of duty, superior to vanity, despisers of
boasting, content to toil in obscurity and shed their
blood at the frontiers of the empire, unrepining at the
cold mistrust of their masters, not clamorous for the
honors so sparingly awarded to them, but satisfied with
the daily work of their hands, and full of faith in the
national destiny which they were daily accomplishing."

In that hard, pagan Roman world, where human life
was made a hell for so many, the harshness in the
career of Julius Caesar is alleviated by the episode
when he slept on the bare floor of his hut, giving his
cot to Oppius, one of his underlings, who was very
ill in the midst of the campaign.

The galaxy of centurions reflect the nobility of character that persisted in their ranks.

There was the centurion who admired the spiritual
worship of monotheistic Israel and erected a syna-

gogue for the Jews in his city. He came to Jesus, seeking healing for one of his servants, who was sick.

There was Cornelius, described as a just man and one that feareth God. He did not allow his exemplary morality to hinder him from repentance when he heard Peter enunciate the wonderful words of life in Christ.

There was Julius, to whose custody Paul was committed on that final journey to Rome and the headsman's axe. He refused the suggestion of his associates

that, after the cruel fashion of their age, Paul and the other prisoners be slain lest they escape at the time of the shipwreck. He is remembered with favor because he courteously entreated the apostle and gave him liberty.

The centurion to whom was given supervision of the crucifixion was not wanting in that same nobility of character. He stood there in pronounced contrast to the ordinary soldiers, decadent in morals, jeering, jesting, gambling. It was his superiority in moral character that permitted him to perceive the spiritual excellence, transcending the category of the mortal, in the character of Jesus. "Deep was calling to deep." Had his nature been gross and hard and intensely materialistic, self-centered, and crude, he would not have been able to find in Jesus the beauty that he should desire Him.

I.   Our Reasons for Belief in the Deity of Christ

Before we consider some of the reasons compelling

the centurion to reach his conviction concerning the divine nature of the Crucified, we do well to examine the manifold bases which we marshal to support our belief in the deity of Jesus. There are the miracles which authenticated His claims and disclosed His eternal power and Godhead. There is the virgin birth, by which He entered our world, and the supernatural acts by which He displayed His power over the forces of nature, disease, demons, and death.

There is the evidence of the art, which is worthy of a god, in that which He omitted. Nathaniel Hawthorne in *The Scarlet Letter* portrays with masterful strokes the character of Hester Prynne. In that superb study of the psychology of guilt, he never once brought her openly to the place of repentance for her sin. If he had done so, he would have been pursuing the hackneyed course of the sentimental, moralizing stories so prevalent in the pious circles of his age. It is by what he refused to do that he displays his consummate artistry and genius as a novelist. Thomas de Quincy observed that the difficulty of a critic reading a book is in discovering what an author ingeniously omitted. Carlyle said that there was a rich harvest for the man who will ponder the silences of Cromwell. Think of the occasions when Jesus declined to perform miracles for His selfish purposes. He refused to turn stones into bread and appease His hunger at the behest of Satan. He refrained from supplying His own need of food by miraculous methods in contrast to occasions when in compassion for the hungering multitudes He had multiplied the loaves and fishes. He refused to summon twelve legions of angels to deliver Him from the clutches of His enemies and the nails of the cross itself. He rejected answering the questions of those who interrogated Him in idle curiosity. He refused with due courtesy the proffered opiate because He would not bandage His eyes as death crept close. There is something amazingly godlike in the restraint of Jesus. There was a mien in Jesus worthy of heaven's eternal king.

King Arthur established his right to royalty when he demonstrated his ability to extract the sword Sxcalibur from the magical stone. By his character and His death, Jesus matched the Old Testament foregleams of the Messiah.

The teachings of Jesus show as well as demand that He be God. Where can one produce parallels to the fourteenth chapter of St. John's Gospel, the Sermon on the Mount, the parables of the Prodigal Son and the Good Samaritan. The ages have followed the astounded natives of Nazareth in asking, "Whence hath this man this wisdom?" The Cambridge scientist Romanes found a convincing argument in the absence from the teachings of Christ of any doctrine which the subsequent growth of human knowledge has had to invalidate and discard.

The Gospel portrait of Christ is an altogether unlikely product of the human imagination. The eloquent New England Unitarian, Theodore Parker, said that it would take a Jesus to forge a Jesus. Rousseau asks the question as to which of the disciples would have been capable of inventing the figure of Jesus.

That those who knew Jesus most intimately were most sure of His deity is a telling testimony to the validity of His claims. An able student of history was wont to counsel, "Do not get too close to your heroes." Those nearest to Jesus evidently found in Him nothing amiss. John, closer to Him than any of the disciples, proclaimed before the world that in Him he beheld the glory of the only-begotten of the Father.

The potent influence for good exerted by Jesus in the world could not have emanated from a psychopathic character or an unabashed impostor or a figment of the imagination of his defrauding or deceived disciples. Few would repudiate Principal A. M. Fairbairn's assertion that Jesus was the most powerful and spiritual force that ever operated for good on and in humanity. As C. Loring Brace concludes in his *Gesta Christ:* "A Being who can lead for all future ages the moral and humane progress of humanity may well claim a respect for His words, no other being can demand."

The charge pressed at the trial, which sent Jesus to His death, was that He claimed to be the Son of God. Everywhere and always He advanced that claim.

In a letter to a friend, Robert Browning asked him to clinch his conviction. The resurrection of Jesus from the dead clinches our conviction concerning His deity. Not many years following that event, which Lyman Abbott said was the best attested in the ancient world, the Apostle Paul in his Epistle to the Romans contended that it was by reason of the resurrection that Jesus was declared to be the Son of God with power.

These are some of the foundations upon which the church has rested her belief in the deity of Jesus.

II.   *Reasons for the Centurion's Conviction Concerning the Deity of Jesus*

What were the particular reasons for the Roman centurion's suddenly expressed faith? Luke records the utterance: "Certainly this was a righteous man." The centurion had been able to perceive innocence, goodness, perfection, symmetry and purity of character in Jesus, such as He had never before witnessed. He recognized Jesus, the Good Paragon, the Crystal Christ of Lanier's portrait of Him. He was moved profoundly by the behavior of Jesus as He faced death. There was majesty and magnanimity and serenity, whereas in all others there was malignity and malice and frenzy and vile imprecations. The centurion may well have been fascinated by the trilingual placard which Pilate would not allow to be removed as it announced, "Jesus of Nazareth, the King of the Jews." This Roman had attended other crucifixions, where men had passed to the gates of death shouting oaths and curses at their executioners and judges. Never before had he heard a prayer for their forgiveness. Without exception, the victims of crucifixion had received the anaesthetic furnished by the philanthropic women of Jerusalem. Jesus, with becoming graciousness, remained aloof from merciful drugs. The centurion listened closely, we can suppose, to the tender words addressed by Jesus to His mother. In the apt comment of the late Dr. James H. Snowden, of Western Theological Seminary, Pittsburgh, "This scene must have deeply affected the Roman: he had never before known the hard crust of that age to bear such a tender blossom." He caught the commanding, confident words of finale in which the victim emerged the victor, saying "It is Finished!" He was subdued in spirit by the committal prayer of the spirit, which accompanied the last, ineffable, homeward sigh of the soul that men call death. He was awed by the preternatural darkness that fell like a mantle over the scene at the place of the skull. He felt the reeling earth, suggesting that behind the dim unknown standeth God, within the shadows, keeping watch above His own. All was still. There on the central cross was Christ, whose dying crimson like a robe spread o'er His body on the tree. It was out of a heart which knew the dawn of faith, that the centurion cried, "Truly this was the Son of God."

III.   *The Cross and the Deity of Jesus.*

The centurion had emphasized the fact which clothes the cross with meaning, namely, the deity of Jesus.

The cross is only the emblem of another martyr, with no relevance to our soul's terrible need if the One who suffered and died there were not very God, King of all the ages, robed in light ere worlds began. It was necessary if the death of Jesus were to satisfy divine justice and be a sacrifice of infinite value that He be God and man. That which the centurion enunciated by his confession, however dim his faith, was essential if there were to be an atonement by which forgiveness was made possible and available. "He only could un-lock the gate of heaven and let us in."

As faith in the cross without acknowledgment of the deity of Jesus is impossible, so faith in the deity apart from faith in the cross is inadequate. If Jesus were the Son of God and not the Mediator, who died to expiate for our guilt, that would be poor comfort indeed. If the incarnation were designed to solve our deepest problem, that of sin and guilt, there must have been the atonement, which our blessed Redeemer procured by shedding His blood for the remission of sins.

The fundamental fact on which the cross and the faith of the Christian rest is the deity of Jesus. The message of the gospel leads beyond that fact to the wondrous love of the Son of God in His redeeming death. "For God so loved the world, that he gave his only begotten Son, that whosoever believeth in him should not perish, but have everlasting life." "Herein is love, not that we loved God, but that he loved us, and sent his Son to be the propitiation for our sins."

Are you living in the conviction of the centurion that Jesus, who died on the cross, was the everlasting Son of the Father? Moreover are you living in that ampler creed of the great apostle, who declared that he lived "by the faith of the Son of God, who loved me, and gave Himself for me"?

13

Chosen in the Stead of Judas

*"The lot fell upon Matthias;
and he was numbered with the eleven apostles."*
ACTS 1:26

It was the first election to be held in the history of the Christian church. The remaining disciples, acting on the advice of Peter, exercised reason and common sense and then prayed for divine guidance. Out of a large number of possible candidates among the followers of Jesus during His public ministry, two men, Matthias and Joseph called Barsabas, whose surname was Justus, were chosen. The disciples resorted to the ancient practice, still pursued in some Mennonite circles, of casting lots. They cast lots with the supplication that God would be pleased to direct their choice. The lot fell upon Matthias and he was numbered with the eleven apostles.

Apart from the casting of lots, the other aspects of the disciples' method constitute a pattern for us in the many decisions with which we are confronted as individuals. We must use the reason, common sense, and the powers of judgment with which God has endowed us, lifting the earnest prayer that His directing hand will be upon us, controlling our minds and overruling all of the circumstances involved in the particular situation.

Matthias was the successor of Judas Iscariot.

Pascal, the French physicist, philosopher, and exponent of the Augustinian theology, observed that one of the superior features of the New Testament is the complete absence of all vitriol and vituperation in its references to those who had a part in accomplishing the crucifixion of Jesus. Perhaps Peter was recalling all too vividly his own precarious and indeed derelict position on that dark betrayal night, when he exercised such marked restraint in his allusion to the shame and tragedy of Judas. It is with a charity approximating tenderness that he speaks of Judas "which was guide to them that took Jesus."

He gives the laconic utterance that Judas went "to his own place." In that reserved yet pronounced statement we observe how in this world we, in a sense, determine our place in the hereafter. In the mysterious control which the sovereign God exercises over us, inciting us both to will and to do His good pleasure, some are enabled to choose Christ as their portion. Under the impetus of God's Spirit, they are filled with a desire to attain unto the heavenly life through the merits and mediation of Christ. To them belongs the promise of the place prepared by our Saviour. Others, while in this life, decide to go out into the darkness of a Christless eternity, refusing to accept Christ as their Saviour. The persons who do not enter the blessedness of Heaven will be those who have no desire to be there. They would find there no congenial atmosphere. Heaven would not prove a homelike atmosphere for the attitudes and characters which they have developed in this world. They would not be at home with the Lord nor would they be compatible with the spiritual surroundings which are inevitable in His holy presence. Even as Judas went to his own place, every one of us will go to his fitting place.

Matthias was called to be the successor of Judas. I recall a clergyman who once remarked to me, "It is easier to succeed a sinner than a saint." In a measure that may be true, but it must be added that the lowering of the standards of an office by one who has regarded it unworthily, meanly, or as a very little thing, and the consequent loss of respect for the position incurred because of one who brought his rank into disrepute, tend to make the task onerous for one who has been called to succeed him. He has to struggle to regain respect for his office. There is a misfortune in having an ignoble predecessor. An unworthy progenitor casts a blight over his posterity and renders it difficult for them to enjoy the prestige which otherwise might be theirs in society. The head of a business firm, who has brought discredit upon his company, imposes a burden which it is difficult indeed for those who succeed to his executive chair to remove, especially in respect to public relations. When the leader of an educational institution allows his own character to be sullied, the reflection somehow rests on his school. The man who follows him has a fight to regain the confidence of students, faculty, and alumni. The leader of a nation, who, like Jeroboam has caused the country to sin and has demonstrated openly his unfitness to lead the destinies of his people, often leaving the country in virtual shambles, compels his successors in office to meet a demoralized and disenchanted citizenry, who must be disabused of sinister and fallacious philosophies, and the reaping of the whirlwind of moral and political disorder. Sometimes in a church a new pastor must confront a disaffected people, saddened and disillusioned by the blunders of his predecessor and quite disposed to be suspicious of the integrity and competence of any new leadership.

There is a fine art of being a good predecessor so that those who come after us will not be entering into the harvest of our faults and mistakes, but rather the fruit of our high ideals and devoted labors.

Peter was eager to have the niche occupied by Judas filled by another before the descent of the Holy Spirit upon the day of Pentecost. In the Revolutionary battlefield memorial at the field of Saratoga near Schuylerville, New York, there are statues of the several commanders, each occupying a separate niche. There is one niche with a telling vacancy. It symbolizes the career of Benedict Arnold, once a hero, later denounced as a traitor. The niche occupied by Judas Iscariot was not permitted to remain vacant. God in His wise and merciful providence arranges to have a bad occupant replaced by a good man. When Saul made shipwreck of his office as king, he was supplanted by David, a man after God's own heart, who was destined to lead Israel in the paths of righteousness, enshrining the ark of the Lord at the heart of the nation's life. Wicked King Ahaz, who led his nation into idolatry, was followed after his death, which concluded a reign of sixteen years, by his son, Hezekiah, who proved to be one of the most admirable and devout of the kings of Judah. Rehoboam, Solomon's unwise and headstrong son, exchanged the shields of gold for shields of brass and led the nation down the road to ruin. His queen, Maacah, survived as a dowager in the reigns of her son and grandson. The patroness of a cult of immorality practiced in the name of religion, she was deposed by her grandson. The son of Rehoboam and Maacah was Abijam, whose short regime was marked by evils similar to those of his iniquitous father. Abijam's son, Asa, was altogether unlike his grandparents and father in moral character. Indeed he was vastly superior ethically to his great-grandfathers, Solomon, who professing himself to be wise became foolish, and Absalom, the vain and rebellious. Asa in his good reign purified the land of idols, became notable as a man of prayer and godliness, and recalled the people to the God whom they had forsaken. God in His wisdom and grace does not cumber the earth with an unbroken lineage of evil leaders. In his grace, whether in the history of nations or families or churches, there is a respite from the ignoble as He raises up noble men and women to fill the very places occupied for a season by those who were base in character.

God does not permit the taints and blunders of one of His servants or an entire generation of His people to arrest the progress of His kingdom in the world. An honored and veteran pastor of the Schwenkfelder church once told me of the period when, as a student of Union Theological Seminary in New York, he served as assistant to Dr. Charles H. Parkhurst at the old Madison Square Presbyterian Church. An outstanding sermon by Dr. Parkhurst, which he recalled to me, was based on the passage in II Samuel, the sixth chapter, where it is related that as the ark, the most sacred object in Israel's national and religious life, was brought out of the house of Abinadab and transported towards Jerusalem, at a rough place in the road, the oxen stumbled and caused the cart on which the ark rested to shake. Even so, said Dr. Parkhurst, fallible men, who help to direct temporal affairs of the church commit gross errors of judgment and conduct, seemingly threatening the continuing existence and influence of the Christian church. None of these things can prevent the church from marching on in strength and zeal towards the day of ultimate triumph. Judas cannot work permanent havoc to the kingdom of Christ. God will raise up a Matthias to fill his post.

Matthias was chosen instead of Joseph called Barsabas. In every election and appointment there is someone who is not chosen. Many times it would seem that the person defeated was better qualified than the person chosen. In these eventualities, where the less competent and worthy, according to our estimate, are advanced above the more gifted and talented, we have to trust that somehow God in His strange, inscrutable, but ever wise providence has controlled the choice. He has some plan in mind by which the apparently poor choice will be best adapted to the scheme of things.

Although Matthias was elevated to an important office in the early church and a post of honor enjoyed by few, his name never thereafter appears in the New Testament record.

The minister of a nationally known church told me that he congratulated those elected to offices in his parish on the day of their election because so many, having arrived at that distinction, seemed to vanish. It was as though they looked upon the election as a consummation and reward rather than as a summons to further and wider service. In a remarkable survey of American theology from the middle of the last century into the second and third decades of the present century, the author, Dr. Frank Hugh Foster, tells how it would be well for many pastors to bid farewell to persons uniting with their churches on the very date of their reception into membership, because instead of viewing that ceremony as the beginning of what ought to be a useful relationship, they disappear as though they have finished a transaction.

On the other hand, Matthias may have been a quiet, unspectacular soul, whose loyal activity attracted no attention. Such persons often prove to be bulwarks of strength.

The silence concerning Matthias does suggest that there are persons who simply occupy an office. They are incumbents, completely subordinated to a station. It is said that Queen Victoria once wrote to a clergyman whom she had appointed bishop of Rochester declaring that she hoped his new office would not result in his ruin as a preacher. She indicated that she had noticed that most bishops, save the bishop of St. Albans, her beloved Dr. W. Boyd Carpenter, never preached so well after their elevation to the episcopacy. They became engrossed in administrative responsibilities and their voices no longer spoke vividly for Christ and His kingdom. Many occupy positions and have as their sole distinction the fact that they are incumbents, whereas others bring lustre and honor to less conspicuous roles.

Above all, as Peter pointed out, Matthias was chosen to be a witness of the resurrection of Christ. It was a requisite, as the Acts of the Apostles informs us, that the man who was chosen should be one of the men "which have companied with us all the time that the

Lord Jesus went in and out among us, beginning from the baptism of John, unto the same day that he was taken up from us." In order to be considered a suitable witness of the resurrection one had to have knowledge of and fellowship with Jesus from the beginning of His public ministry when He identified Himself with the sinful world He was to redeem by being baptized of John at the Jordan.

In order to bear office in the Christian church today and indeed to be one of its members, one should have a certain familiar friendship with Jesus, believing in Him as the incarnate Son of God, whom it behooved to fulfill all righteousness and who assumed the burden of our guilt at His baptism, dying for our sins on the cross, in a perfect sacrifice accepted of God that we might have the remission of our sins, rising from the dead in power and great glory, making available to men in their sins and needs the wondrous power of the cross.

I invite all of you who know friendship with the Lord Jesus, who believe in His resurrection from the dead, hence His incarnation and His deity, and have felt the power of His resurrection in your lives, to decide that you will assume your place of fidelity and service in His church. Thus you will appear before the world as witnesses of the resurrection, friends of the Lord Jesus, who travel in His dear company and in that of His friends.

14

The Man Who Was Not Elected

"And they appointed two, Joseph called Barsabas, who was surnamed Justus, and Matthias. And they gave forth their lots; and the lot fell upon Matthias." ACTS 1:23, 26

In the New Testament there is an eminent company of the otherwise obscure, who attained a strange kind of immortality because they passed momentarily under the brilliant light of the inspired chronicler. Simeon the venerable appears long enough to embrace the infant Christ and recite his own swansong. Gaius was immortalized by a single stroke of the pen of St. Paul's amanuensis, Tertius, when the apostle characterized him as "mine host, and of the whole church." Andronica and Junia have had their memory perpetuated in the touching allusion of the apostle: "my kinsmen and my fellow prisoners who are of note among the apostles, who also were in Christ before me." There is Theophilus, to whom Luke addressed the Gospel and the Acts of the Apostles. Sergius Paulus is remembered because he was provincial governor of Paphos when Paul and Barnabas tarried there.

In this company one would include Joseph called Barsabas.

Following the ascension of our Lord, the disciples assembled in the upper room, hallowed by recent sacred memories, and there awaited the effusion of the Holy Spirit at Pentecost. Peter called the first congregational meeting. The purpose of the meeting was to elect a successor of Judas. Two men were proposed. Both were recognized in the church as faithful, honorable, and devoted. Both were witnesses of the fact of the resurrection of Jesus. After a period of prayer, the apostles resorted to the ancient method of casting lots. The lot fell upon Matthias. We never hear about him again. What of Joseph called Barsabas, a man who was considered but missed being enrolled in the glorious company of the apostles?

Stephen A. Douglas, who bore the sobriquet, "Little Giant," and on whose property the campus of the University of Chicago now stands, was overheard exclaiming as his latest moment drew nigh, "I missed it." Could he have been alluding to the election of 1860 when Lincoln defeated him? Was he harboring throughout the residue of his career a deep resentment of that defeat, although he had, with a dramatic gesture, held the hat of Lincoln at his inaugural in 1861?

Two were proposed. One was chosen. "Know ye not," asks St. Paul, "that they that run in a race run all, but one receiveth the prize?"

One wonders how Joseph called Barsabas, whose name seems to indicate that he was born on the Sabbath, reacted to his defeat.

The company of Joseph called Barsabas have not been without paens of sympathy from the poets. Walt Whitman exclaimed that he did not play marches for accepted victors only, but great marches for conquered and slain persons, generals that lost engagements, and all overcome heroes and the numberless unknown heroes, equal to the greatest heroes known. The American expatriate in Rome, William Wetmore Story, sang the hymn of the conquered, who fell in the battle of life — who died overwhelmed in the strife, who strove and failed, acting bravely a silent and desperate part. He concludes that those whom the world called victors and who won the success of a day do not appear in that light when history unrolls her long annals.

Joseph, called Barsabas, could have allowed himself to become embittered and warped in personality.

One recalls Aaron Burr, having one of the keenest intellects of any figure in American history, twice thwarted in his race for the presidency and the office of governor of New York, latterly passing through an ignoble succession of melancholy chapters, including the tragic duel with Alexander Hamilton, the conspiracy against our government, and the forlorn old age on Staten Island.

There was George B. McClellan, defeated by Lincoln in his race for the presidency and dismissed as commander of the Union Army. Professor William Starr Meyer, of Princeton, in his biography of McClellan speaks of the unhappiness that beclouded his life, saying: "He was in a way one of the worst subordinates and best superiors, that ever lived. As a subordinate, he was restless, critical, often ill at ease, and seemingly unwilling to cooperate with his colleagues or superiors. He knew what was best and others were in his estimation ignorant or insincere. Or he seemed to have the proverbial chip always poised on his cultivated and aristocratic shoulders, the latter for the most part carefully adorned with the proper insignia of his rank and military station."

One thinks of Horace Greeley, the New York journalist. In 1872 a veritable conspiracy of hostile events seemed designed to accomplish his destruction. On October 30 his wife died. Six days thereafter he met defeat as a candidate for the presidency. He retired to his office at the New York Tribune where he was soon supplanted as his mind went into eclipse. On November 29 he died. His grief and disappointment were more than he could bear.

One can accept disappointment and defeat gracefully or allow it to blight and blast his life.

I.

As we recall Joseph called Barsabas whose surname was Justus, we are led to observe that personal worth and greatness are more to be desired than honors and prominent position.

History repeatedly confirms the comment of the author of the Book of Ecclesiastes, when he said: "The race is not to the swift, nor the battle to the strong."

The ablest man, albeit the man who will make the most lasting impact on his own and later generations, is not necessarily occupying the most conspicuous and famous post. A man of superior intellect, cultivation, and spirituality may be overlooked and a man of meager intellectual and moral qualifications advanced to a station of fame and honor.

In the heart of Harrisburg, Pennsylvania, there stands an historic Lutheran church, which was the scene of the Whig convention in 1839. There Henry Clay was defeated and William Henry Harrison, a War of 1812 hero, who with advancing years had receded to the minor office of a county clerk in Ohio, was brought forth and nominated. John Tyler was so incensed by what had transpired that he wept with grief, although he was named as vice president and thus succeeded Harrison who died a month after he had taken office. Clay, when notified of his defeat in Washington, exclaimed in protest and consternation: "Damn them! Damn them! I knew it! My friends are not worth the powder it would take to blow them up."

In that general era of our history, our three ablest statesmen were Webster, Clay and Calhoun. Not one of them ever became president. Historians will agree generally that those who were chosen were inferior in ability to the overlooked triumvirate.

In his *Men who Missed It,* the late Dr. Clarence Edward Macartney contends that there are no ten presidents who can match for ability, brilliancy of mind and distinguished public service such men as Clay, Seward, Webster, Calhoun, Chase, Greeley, McClellan, Blaine, Bryan, and LaFollette, all thwarted on the road to the White House.

In the history of the office of poet laureate in Great Britain there appeared many men whose names and poetry are in oblivion. Few could quote a line from Sir Alfred Ausen, the poet laureate, but virtually everyone in the English speaking world could quote from Rudyard Kipling, who was never awarded that honor.

The fame which surrounds a position of power is at best fleeting. Ellen Glasgow in her delightful autobiography, *The Woman Within,* says that America has a single track mind with respect to her heroes, being able to have only one hero at a time. That observation is questionable, when we recall the large company of heroic figures who won simultaneous popular admiration at so early a date in our history as the War of 1812. We have had a pronounced tendency to demote and forget our heroes. Such a fate befell the heroes of the Spanish-American War. The nation was stirred temporarily by the sensation of the youthful son of a Presbyterian college president slapping the face of a well-known superior officer. Admiral Dewey was lionized and then visited with a wave of popular disfavor. The manager of the Algonquin Hotel in New York in his interesting book, *The Tales of a Wayward Inn,* tells of the day when one of his hotel's most renowned guests, Admiral Winfield S. Schley, dropped dead on a Manhattan street. Although his name had been a household word in America during the Spanish-American War a little more than a decade earlier, his body lay unidentified in a police station for a matter of hours.

In an age when the cult of mediocrity is in the ascendancy, we should be glad to place the accent on personal worth, ability, and character rather than on position and prominence.

II.

The case of Joseph called Barsabas suggests, although we have no knowledge of such a development in his life, that recognition temporarily withheld may be bestowed at a later date.

Today's best sellers among books may not survive a decade as volumes of popularity or significance, whereas a volume quite unnoticed at its appearance may emerge belatedly as a recognized classic. In his own century the writings of the Danish philosopher, Sören Kierkegaard, were accorded little note. After almost three decades of our own century, Kierkegaard's writings became among the most widely quoted and used in the intellectual and theological world. Herman Melville's books loom much larger in our century than in the previous one in which his lot was cast.

Works of art have been overlooked in the life and times of an artist, only to become priceless long after he has died in penury.

Among the gems of English preaching in our century are the sermons of Percy C. Ainsworth, a Wesleyan, who died of typhoid while in his thirties in the early years of the century, never having occupied a notable pulpit nor enjoyed the inspiration of vast congregations.

The published letters of Marcus Dods reveals that six years after the completion of his seminary course when he preached as a supply in innumerable churches, he never once received a call. What despair dogged his footsteps in those unwanted years, when he was unknown to the deserved fame proceeding to him from the publication of his monumental commentaries on Genesis, John's Gospel, and Judges, not to mention other masterful works.

The absence of recognition and popular acclaim mean very little when the years and even the centuries are weighed against the hours. If our work is not given credit here upon the homely earth, then it will be yonder worlds away.

There are compensations in the frustrations similar to that known by Joseph called Barsabas. Very often one is enabled to achieve what he could never have wrought in the coveted position.

Jonathan Edwards, forced out of his pastorate at Northampton where he had followed his grandfather, Solomon Stoddard, was able amid the solitude of the frontier village of Stockbridge in western Massachusetts, where he served as a missionary to the Indians, to write his celebrated treatise on *The Freedom of the Will.*

In exile from France, where he fell into political disrepute, Victor Hugo in a sequestered haven, wrote his famous critique of Shakespeare.

Dismissed from his position in the Salem, Massachusetts, custom house, Nathaniel Hawthorne was, as his wife said that he would be, able to write his remarkable novels.

In the introduction to Frank Hugh Foster's biography of the Andover, Massachusetts, theologian, Edward Amasa Park, it is said that it had been expected that Foster, who later resided in Oberlin, Ohio, would follow Dr. Park in the chair of theology. It was felt that some disappointment must have come to Dr. Foster when that call did not come. However, he wrote later among other works his *Genetic History of New England Theology* and *The Modern Movement in American Theology.* It might have been that Foster, in the particular professor's chair for which he seemed destined for a little while, could never have realized the literary productivity for which he is now recognized in the theological world.

Our frustrations are generally attended by their brighter compensations — the books we have written, the people whom we have met and influenced for good, the opportunities for productive leisure and research, the cultural activities, the wayside ministries of kindness, the added time for family and friends.

Our frustrations remind us of our own inadequacies. However we may excel, there are always the deficiencies in us. They are in the very area where others are highly proficient and talented. There are positions which at times allure us but for which we would find ourselves wanting in requisite endowments and experience.

Plutarch, the first great biographer in many respects, told of a defeated candidate in Athens, returning home and remarking that it did him good to see that there were three hundred men in that city who were better men than he. The Apostle Paul encouraged the spirit of humility as he enjoined, "In honor preferring one another," "Let nothing be done through strife or vainglory; but in lowliness of mind let each esteem other better than themselves. Look not every man on his own things, but every man also on the things of others." (Phil. 2:3, 4)

We must seek to recognize the hand of God in our frustrations. James G. Blaine said with a measure of resignation, "I am fated not to be president." When defeat was several times visited upon William Jennings

Bryan, he quoted the Scriptures: "The lot is cast into the lap; but the whole disposing thereof is of the Lord."

No matter how incommensurate with your capabilities is your place and how inadequate a theatre for the manifestation of your talents it may seem, God in His wise providence has you in the place where He wills you to be and where you are most fitted to serve His cause. As Browning puts it in Rabbi Ben Ezra:

> All I could never be
> All men ignored in me
> This I was worth to God.

We should rejoice in any humble place in the Saviour's service. Jeremiah counselled his nephew and secretary, "Seekest thou great things for thyself? Seek them not." Let us be grateful for the privilege, however limited, of serving our Master, who came among us as One that serveth, "not to be ministered unto, but to minister, and to give his life a ransom for many."